Issues

Issues

A Resource of Play Scripts and Activities for Teachers

Second Edition

Hazel Edwards

Published in 2023 by Amba Press, Melbourne, Australia
www.ambapress.com.au

© Hazel Edwards 2023

All rights reserved. No part of this book may be reproduced or transmitted in any form or by any means, electronic or mechanical, including photocopying, recording or by any information storage and retrieval system, without prior permission in writing from the publisher.

First published in 1991 by Jacaranda Press
This edition was published in 2023

Cover design – Tess McCabe
Proofreader – Megan Bryant

ISBN: 9781922607768 (pbk)
ISBN: 9781922607775 (ebk)

A catalogue record for this book is available from the National Library of Australia.

These scripts have been workshopped in schools and checked by the appropriate health practitioners.

Acknowledgements of Earlier Publications

Wrong Rhymes was earlier published in *Primary Plays* by Nelson in 1981.

The Bunga Berry Pavlova Dream with Whipped Cream was first published in *More Primary Plays* by Nelson in 1981 and subsequently in NSW School Magazine several times. This has been published here with permission of Five Senses.

The Parts of Speech TV Show was frequently performed at Holmesglen Institute as part of Diploma of Professional Writing by adult literacy programs and students. The variation Acting Parts of Speech was originally published by Phoenix in 2018. Parts of Speech has been published here with permission of Five Senses.

Inside Outside In was published in *Re-Enact Secondary* by Phoenix in 2018. Inside Outside In (Anorexia) has been published here with permission of Five Senses.

Sleuth Astrid: The Mind Reading Chook has been adapted from Hazel Edwards' eBook *Sleuth Astrid: The Mind Reading Chook,* illustrated by Jane Connory. *Astrid the Mind Reading Chook* was originally published by Macmillan Education Australia as a part of the Cracker series.

Sleuth Astrid: Lost Voice of the Grand Final adapted from Hazel Edwards' eBook *Sleuth Astrid: Lost Voice of the Grand Final,* illustrated by Jane Connory.

Other scripts from *Issues* originally published by Jacaranda Press in 1991.

Contents

About the Author	vii
Introduction	1
Wrong Rhymes – A script about inclusion	3
Inside Outside In – An audio play about anorexia nervosa	13
The Umbrella Trees with Weak Knees – A conservation spoof	25
She's Not Here Any More – A script about the death of a classmate	35
The Galactic Gossipmongers – A futuristic look at peer group pressure and highly contagious disease	45
Putting It On – A script about haemophilia	55
The House of X – A script about prejudice	61
Colours – A script with a colourful approach to prejudice	69
The Bunga-Berry Pavlova Dream with Whipped Cream – A melodrama about a country town initiative to attract tourists	77

The Parts of Speech TV Show – A script about finding the
right words in difficult situations   87

Sleuth Astrid: The Mind Reading Chook – A simple satire with
complex ideas for gifted students   99

Sleuth Astrid: Lost Voice of the Grand Final – A play about
celebrations and the influence of sport   115

Contacts and Further Information   135

> **Forewarning:** Some of the issues and topics raised in this book can be confronting. Please contact Beyond Blue, 1300 22 4636, www.beyondblue.org.au or LifeLine, 13 11 14, www.lifeline.org.au if you or a student needs additional support. You can also talk to your GP or another allied health professional about these topics.

About the Author

Hazel Edwards, OAM, is an award-winning author of books for children, teachers and adults.

An avid reader, as a young girl, Hazel Edwards wrote her first novel in grade six, a mystery about adventurous children stuck in a mine. This passion for writing continued after working in a secondary school and lecturing at teachers' college.

Aged twenty-seven, Hazel published her first novel, *General Store*, a book based on life in a rural town. It is Hazel's third published work that is her best known, the children's picture book classic, *There's a Hippopotamus on Our Roof Eating Cake*. This special imaginary friend has been cherished by children and parents alike and led to the dubious honour of Hazel being referred to as 'the Hippo Lady'.

Since its publication in 1980, the ageless *There's a Hippopotamus on Our Roof Eating Cake* has been reprinted annually, evolved into a series of seven picture books, inspired a junior chapter book, classroom play scripts, a musical stage production and a short movie. The Hippopotamus books have also been translated into Mandarin, Braille and Auslan signing for the hearing impaired and were presented as an official Australian Government gift to the children of Princess Mary of Denmark.

Whilst Hazel loves creating quirky, feisty characters for independent readers in her easy-to-read junior chapter books, she writes for all ages and has published over 220 books across a range of subjects and genres.

Published titles include *f2m:the boy within*, the first co-written young adult novel about gender transition and picture book *Stickybeak*.

Hazel has collaborated with experts to publish adult non-fiction titles such as such as *Difficult Personalities* (translated into seven languages), and helps people craft interesting memoirs and family histories in her popular workshops based on her book *Writing a Non-Boring Family History*. More recently a 'Complete Your Book in a Year' course has been offered via Zoom.

Awarded the Australian Antarctic Division Arts Fellowship (2001), Hazel travelled to Casey Station on the 'Polar Bird' ice-ship. This visit inspired a range of creative projects including the young adult eco-thriller *Antarctica's Frozen Chosen*, picture book *Antarctic Dad* and the memoir *Antarctic Writer on Ice*, as well as classroom playscripts.

A fan of interesting and unusual locations, Hazel has been a guest writer-in-residence in communities across Australia, a visiting author to Pasir Ridge International School in Indonesia and an author ambassador to Youfu West Street International School in China.

Passionate about literacy and creativity, Hazel has mentored gifted children and proudly held the title of Reading Ambassador for various organisations. Formerly a director on the Committee of Management of the Australian Society of Authors, Hazel was awarded an OAM for Literature in 2013. She is the patron of the Society of Women Writers (Vic) and in 2022 she was awarded the Monash University Distinguished Alumni Award for Education.

Introduction

Using scripts in schools enables topical issues to be discussed in a reassuring and accessible way. All scripts within this resource have been workshopped in schools and checked by the appropriate health practitioners. This book also provides a series of discussion prompts and activities for each script. They can be used as extension for a lesson, or used to continue to tease out or dip deeper into an issue or a topic.

Scripts allow hesitant students to be able to assume the protection of a character and play a role or explore issues which may concern them in real life, like inclusion, prejudice, or fears about infection. Sometimes the character is an animal, tree, colour or abstraction and that enables further distancing and a freedom to explore. Educators can cast the same play multiple times so the student can play different roles and gain other perspectives on the same situation.

Scripts are time savers for educators, enabling both the content and literacy skills to be used. These scripts usually contain a chorus, some non-speaking parts and/or a narrator to link and provide parts with a range of reading and acting skills. To be part of a chorus you may not have to read much dialogue aloud, but you are involved in the issues, the performance and are part of the group. It's a significant new experience for some.

The bonus is when students learn to group craft their own scripts based on topical issues in their world. They extend their writing and reading skills but also their confidence. They learn to model non-human casts like trees. Most of all they learn to explore issues from a different perspective.

The discussion suggestions and activities encourage students to take topical issues further by finding out facts (research), debating, using proof not just opinion and maybe performing with film, puppetry, stand up or cosplay.

As settings and costumes are simple, time-poor educators are attracted to try the script experience within a period. If a subject turns out to be popular and highly relevant to the broader school community, it can be performed for them too, maybe with more dressing up or props.

All these scripts have been workshopped in schools with real students. Most have subtext or more serious issues underneath the apparently simple words and fun. But they are not didactic nor propagandist for any issue, rather they are meant to open discussion on varied ways to solve problems and issues in today's school communities.

This is the aim of this script collection, to provide skills to explore topical issues in a way which is fun but informative for everyone.

Wrong Rhymes

A script about inclusion

Cast

- Storyteller, holds a big book
- Mice, three, without tails
- Pigs, four
- Bears, Mother, Father and Baby Bear, each with a porridge bowl
- Goldilocks
- Cats, any number, but one with a violin
- Dogs, any number, but one with a bone
- Big Bad Wolf, with a black cloak and a white cloak
- Little Red Riding Hood, with three different hoods or scarves – red, green and yellow
- Sheep, any number

Props

- Big book labelled 'My Story'
- Porridge bowls for bears
- Violin

- Bone
- Black hood and white hood for wolf
- Hoods or scarves for Red Riding Hood
- Tissues for wolf
- 'The End' and 'Tail End' signs

Setting

- Anywhere, but with a chair aside for the Storyteller

Wrong Rhymes Script

(Storyteller speaks to the audience, holding a book in front of him.)

STORYTELLER   Once upon a time … a long, long time ago … in a faraway place, there lived …
(Animals rush on stage and interrupt. Each bows to the audience as it speaks. Wolf waits at the back.)

MICE   Three blind mice. That's us.

PIGS   Three little pigs. That's us.

BEARS   A Father Bear, a Mother Bear and a Baby Bear. That's us.

SHEEP   Some black sheep. Baa baa black sheep. That's us.

CATS   Cats. We're the cats from 'hey diddle diddle, the cat and the fiddle'.

DOGS   Dogs. We were Old Mother Hubbard's dogs. We like food from the cupboard.
(Wolf swirls his black cape.)

WOLF   *(Loudly)* And I am The Big Bad Wolf!
(All animals jump back in fright. Storyteller shuts the book.)

STORYTELLER   No. No. You've got it all wrong. This is my story. It is different. You don't belong in my story. You belong in other stories and nursery rhymes. Someone else created you.
(Turns to the Wolf.)
Did you come from the story of 'Peter and the Wolf'?

WOLF   *(Wolf rubs his tummy and shakes his head.)*
No. That was my cousin.

ANIMALS	*(Together)* Did you come from the story of 'The Three Little Pigs'? *(Wolf huffs and puffs at the pigs, then shakes his head.)*
WOLF	No. That was my big brother. *(Pigs look happier.)*
ANIMALS	*(Together)* Did you come from the story of 'Little Green Riding Hood'?
STORYTELLER	*(Surprised)* Green Riding Hood? Wasn't it Little Red Riding Hood? *(Little Red Riding Hood comes out, carrying three hoods.)*
RIDING HOOD	I like a change. *(She tries on different hoods.)* Everyone has heard the story of 'Little Red Riding Hood'. They've heard it so many times I decided to change it. Sometimes I'm 'Little Green Riding Hood'. Sometimes I'm 'Little Yellow Riding Hood' It just depends upon how I feel. Or who I'm with. Sometimes I want to blend in and be included. Other times I want to be different. I like to choose. *(She turns to Wolf.)* But I don't trust you or your big brother!
WOLF	That was my uncle.
STORYTELLER	The big bad wolf doesn't belong in my story at all.
ANIMAL CHORUS	*(Singing mockingly.)* Who's afraid of The Big Bad Wolf, The Big Bad Wolf. The Big Bad Wolf. Who's afraid of The Big Bad Wolf? Tra, la, la, la, la. Go home Wolf. We don't want you.

WOLF	That's not fair. I always get the blame. But it was my cousin, or my big brother, or my uncle. And once the big bad wolf was my baby brother. Nobody gives me a chance.
DOGS	Not even a stray dogs' chance. *(Wolf leaves sadly, crying into his tissues.)*
STORYTELLER	I'll start again. Once upon a time … a long, long time ago … in a place far away from here … there lived … *(Goldilocks races on stage. She pulls three bears forward.)*
GOLDILOCKS	It must be a bear story. Here's Father Bear.
FATHER BEAR	I'm Father Bear. I have a great big chair, and a great big bed, and … this great big bowl of yucky porridge. Why can't we have muesli or cornflakes for a change?
STORYTELLER	No. It's not your turn. You're the wrong animal. *(Turns to Goldilocks.)* Goldilocks, come and take him away. He belongs to your story, not to mine. *(Father Bear steps back, pretending to eat porridge and pulling faces at the taste. Mother Bear comes forward.)*
MOTHER BEAR	Once upon a time, there was a mother bear. That's me. I have a middle sized chair and a middle sized bed. I also have a bowl of cold porridge. For breakfast, I'd rather have bacon and eggs.
PIGS	Bacon! Where does she think the bacon comes from?
MOTHER BEAR	Sorry, Pigs.

GOLDILOCKS	Mother Bear has a middle-sized part in my story.
STORYTELLER	*(Trying to push bears off stage.)* But she hasn't got a part in my story. Mother Bear is the wrong character.
MOTHER BEAR	You don't have to push. I hate rude people. *(Mother Bear upends the bowl of porridge over the storyteller's head.)* Never forget Mother Bear! *(Storyteller wipes off porridge. Cats help by licking him.)*
STORYTELLER	Once upon a time … *(Baby Bear tugs at Storyteller.)* What is it? Do you want some porridge? Ask your mother. She seems to have too much.
BABY BEAR	Once upon a time, there was a baby bear. I had a baby chair. And a baby bed. And a baby bowl of porridge, but she ate it all up. *(Points to Goldilocks)*
DOGS	She did what?
STORYTELLER	Everyone has their problems.
SHEEP	We don't. We just do what everybody else does.
STORYTELLER	My problem is how to tell my story.
ANIMAL CHORUS	And it isn't a bear story. Go away bears. Take your porridge with you. *(Bears dance away with Goldilocks, then they bend over to reveal 'The End' pinned on their backsides. They stay in the background.)*
STORYTELLER	I hope that's the end of the bears.
PIGS	*(Pigs come forward.)* What about us? In lots of stories, we are VIPs.

MICE	What does that mean?
DOGS	Very important pigs.
1ST PIG	I'm the pig from Tom, Tom the Piper's son.
CATS	Didn't you get eaten? *(Pig ignores the cats.)*
PIGS	We're the three pigs who built their houses.
1ST PIG	I built my house of straw
2ND PIG	I built my house of wood.
3RD PIG	I built my house of bricks.
PIGS	*(Together)* And along came the big, bad wolf. *(Wolf puts his head around the corner.)*
WOLF	That was my cousin again. It wasn't me. You burnt his tail in the fire. He hasn't been able to sit down for years.
MICE	The farmer's wife cut off our tails. The wolf is lucky because he still has his tail.
STORYTELLER	And I'm trying to tell you my tale, but you won't let me. *(Mice turn around to reveal 'Tail End' stuck on their tails.)*
SHEEP	What about us? We belong in the nursery rhyme. Baa, baa black sheep. Have you any wool? Yes sir, yes sir, three bags full. One for the master and one for the dame. And one for the little boy who lives down the lane.
STORYTELLER	We've heard that before. Mine is a new story.
DOGS	What about us?

ANIMAL CHORUS	You must put us in your story. People will forget us if you don't. Characters need stories to belong to. Include all of us.
STORYTELLER	*(Throws down book.)* All right. All right. I give up. I'll make up a different story. Come and sit down. *(All animals sit at the Storyteller's feet. Wolf watches from the corner of the stage.)* Once upon a time there were some dogs. *(Dogs stand and bow.)* Some cats *(Cats bow.)* Some sheep *(Sheep bow.)* Some mice *(Mice bow.)* Goldilocks *(Curtseys)* Father Bear *(Bows)* Mother Bear *(Bows)* Baby Bear *(Bows)* Little Rainbow Riding Hood *(Bows and puts on all her hoods.)* And a big, GOOD Wolf! *(Wolf dashes across the stage in his white cloak.)* And they all lived together in a secret place called the Storyteller's imagination. One day, something strange happened … *(Storyteller bends and whispers something into one animal's ear. It nods and passes the message onto the next animal. Message goes around the circle. Wolf whispers it to Storyteller.)*
STORYTELLER	*(Smiles)* It isn't quite the same story I started with. When stories are told, they improve along the way. Oh well, that's how you get a good story. Include ideas from everybody. *(All animals stand and bow to the audience. Storyteller stands in front and bows too.)*

Discussion Starters

- Why do so many folktales have a wolf as the 'baddie'?
- Often stories have characters in a set of 3. Why might that be?
- Different cultures often have different versions of a similar story. Can you find two versions of a similar folktale?

Activities

1. Plan a continuous story. Make a circle. Use a pretend microphone (or a real one). Pass it to each speaker in turn. Start with:
   'One day, something strange happened ...'
   2nd person adds a sentence starting with 'Luckily ...'
   3rd person adds a sentence starting with 'Unluckily ...'
   4th person adds 'A very unusual person did something funny ...'
   The last person needs an unusual twist for the end. 'It was all a dream' is not acceptable, challenge them to think of something creative.

2. Prepare to be a stand up comic. Choose one character e.g. the wolf and talk from their point of view for 1 minute.

3. Cosplay is the practice of dressing up as a character from a film, book, or video game. Cosplay = Costume Play. Cosplayers are those who dress up regularly as their favourite characters.
   Dress up in character and explain how you made the outfit and why each item matters to help the story. Interview someone who enjoys cosplay and share the facts you learnt. Write a short news article about either the cosplay event or the cosplayer.

Inside Outside In

An audio play about anorexia nervosa

Cast

- Advertising Agency Chorus
- Mother
- Melaney, a girl in her mid teens
- Narrator
- Exercise Chorus
- Brother
- Friend(s)
- Doctor
- Food Chorus
- Father
- Laxative
- Body chorus (including Nails, Hair, Teeth, Kidneys, Heart, Menstrual Cycle, Fine Body Hair, Brain)
- Sound-effects operator (SFX), to create background noises (which are noted in italics at the beginning of particular speeches)

Inside Outside In Script

ADVERTISING AGENCY CHORUS
(SFX: Pop music.)
Think thin.
In today's world,
To be a success,
You must be slim.

MOTHER *(SFX: The clatter of a dinner table being set.)*
Dinner time!

MELANEY I'm not hungry right now.

NARRATOR Anorexia is self-imposed starvation.

MOTHER Dinner time Melaney!

MELANEY I ate at Gill's place.

EXERCISE CHORUS Exercise is my name.
There are many varieties of me.
Cycling,
Aerobics,
Swimming, among others.
Usually I'm good for you.
But she is doing too much.
And for the wrong reason.

MELANEY I have eaten a biscuit.
Now I must exercise for at least three hours.
Puff. Pant. Puff. Pant.
Puff. Pant. Puff. Pant.
Pedal. Pedal. Pedal.
I must cycle harder.

NARRATOR Anorexia nervosa is an eating disorder that seriously threatens health.

MELANEY I must not eat.
I might lose control.

NARRATOR	Anorexia nervosa is more than loss of appetite.
MELANEY	I feel cold.
BROTHER	It's warm in here Sis.
MELANEY	But I feel cold.
NARRATOR	If there's no other food, the body begins to eat the protective fat from around organs such as the kidneys and ovaries. That's why you feel cold.
FRIEND	Hi Melaney. Do you like my new jeans? They're size 10.
MELANEY	I'm not going to eat, Until I can fit into my favourite blue dress. That's a size 8!
DOCTOR	How do you feel about your size, Melaney?
MELANEY	I feel fat.
BROTHER	But, Sis, you're skinny. If you stand sideways, You disappear.
MELANEY	I feel fat. That's how I see myself.
BROTHER	You need your eyes tested, Or a different mirror.
MELANEY	I don't want to do anything different. I feel in control when I'm not eating.
ADVERTISING AGENCY CHORUS	*(SFX: Pop music.)* Think thin. In today's world, To be a success, You must be slim.

FRIENDS	We are your friends. We're worried about you. Why is not eating meant to be a secret? Everybody knows what you're doing.
MELANEY	Everything has changed. We moved. It's a new school. Mum and Dad aren't getting on. When I'm on a diet, I can control things. I don't want to be fat.
FOOD CHORUS	We're food. Some people just love us. We have many different flavours. Don't you want us?
MELANEY	Food is the enemy. Go away. I will vomit. I will take laxatives. Go away!
FOOD CHORUS	We are not the enemy. You have the problem, not us.
MELANEY	I'm hungry. But I won't eat. If I eat, I'll lose control.
MOTHER	I think I'm going mad. I go to the cupboard and something is missing. Then I know she's been bingeing secretly again.
ADVERTISING AGENCY CHORUS	*(SFX: Pop music.)* Think thin. In today's world, To be a success, You must be slim.

MOTHER AND FATHER	She was such a good student. Did all her homework without being asked. Always got A in every subject.
MELANEY	I don't want to grow up yet. My parents want me to do well. I must be a success.
NARRATOR	What is success?
BROTHER	Getting into the firsts? Being captain? Telling other people what to do? I don't know.
MELANEY	Being the best.
FRIENDS	At what? Dieting to death?
NARRATOR	There's a difference between 'feeling fat' and 'being fat'.
MELANEY	Inside, there is I and me. We are fighting. I want to eat and be ordinary. Me wants to be in control. Me needs laxatives.
MOTHER	What are all those laxative packets doing under your bed? There are dozens of them.
MELANEY	Leave me alone. That's my business. Don't come into my room.
LAXATIVE	Ahhaaaa, I will D.E.H.Y.D.R.A.T.E. her. I am a laxative.
MELANEY	(SFX: Toilet flushing.) You can't stop me.

BODY CHORUS	(*Slowly*) We are the Body Chorus. We're not in very good condition. Let us introduce ourselves, Or what's left of us. Here are the Nails.
NAILS	We're Melaney's Nails. We're too brittle. We used to be strong and shapely. Now we hide. Why is she doing this to us? We're on her side.
BODY CHORUS	And this is Hair.
HAIR	Hello. I'm Hair. I used to be silky. Now I'm dull and stringy. I need protein. Why is she doing this to me? I'm part of her.
BODY CHORUS	Let us introduce Teeth.
TEETH	We're Teeth. Things are going bad around here.
KIDNEYS	We're Kidneys. There are two of us. We can't work properly any more. Why is she starving us? Our protective layer of fat has gone.
HEART	(*SFX: Heart beats, slow and laboured.*) I'm Melaney's heart. I can't work properly any more. My muscle is getting weak.

	I might fail her.
	My rhythm is wrong.
	Why is she starving me?
MELANEY	I still feel cold.
NARRATOR	Loss of fat and muscle tissue make it hard for the body to keep itself warm.
MENSTRUAL CYCLE	I'm Melaney's Menstrual Cycle.
	I'm stopping.
	I'm going on strike.
	My female hormone levels are dropping.
BODY CHORUS	Why is she doing this to us?
FINE BODY HAIR	I'm Fine Body Hair.
	I am growing on her arms and legs.
	I am trying to make up for her heat loss.
MOTHER, FATHER AND BROTHER	
	Let us help you Melaney.
MELANEY	Help means loss of control.
	I don't need help.
	There's nothing wrong with me.
MOTHER	I packed Melaney's lunch.
	Four dry biscuits with Vegemite.
	I know she throws them out.
	So I put a message with them today.
MELANEY	*(SFX: Unwrapping paper)*
	What's this?
	It's in Mum's writing.
	'Hi Melaney. Only throw three of me away today.'
	(Laughs)
	Okay Mum.
	(SFX: Dialling and then ringing of a phone.)

MELANEY	Hi Mum. It's Melaney. I got your message.
MOTHER	We love you for what you are, not the container you come in. You've been to the doctor, haven't you? The receipt was left on the table. You wanted us to know. Are you asking for help ... giving us clues?
MELANEY	I don't know what to do.
DOCTOR	Hi. I'm Doctor Smith. I'm glad you came to see me again. Come to me regularly.
FOOD CHORUS	Eat us. We're not the problem. We're just food.
DOCTOR	Why is losing weight so important to you Melaney?
MELANEY	I'm not sure why ...
MOTHER, FATHER AND BROTHER	What can we do? We love her. We hate to see this happening. What can we do? Is it our fault?
DOCTOR	No. But she does need professional help. As a doctor, I can give you a referral. A nutritionist or a dietitian can help. Support groups can help. But Melaney must admit that she needs help.
MELANEY	I'm not sure.

MOTHER, FATHER AND BROTHER
: We are her family.
: We need support too.
: We look at her getting thinner and weaker.
: But she won't eat.

DOCTOR
: Support groups exist for families too.
: She needs to go into hospital now.
: Her weight is so low, her meals must be supervised.

MELANEY
: I don't want to go into hospital.

MOTHER, FATHER AND BROTHER
: We bought you a poster for your hospital wall.
: It says, 'If I have the determination to starve, I have the determination to do other things.'

MELANEY
: Thanks.
: I never thought of it that way before.

DOCTOR
: In hospital, we will help you to eat.
: We sit with you.
: You rest in bed.
: When you eat, you'll be able to do other things.
: It's up to you.

ADVERTISING AGENCY CHORUS
: *(SFX: Pop music)*
: Think thin.
: In today's world,
: To be a success,
: You must be slim.

MOTHER, FATHER AND BROTHER
: Turn off that radio commercial.
: We've come to the hospital to see you.
: Hey, you look great.
: You've put on weight.

FATHER   I'll see you at home tonight.
                 Get dressed in your best.
                 We'll do something special.

ADVERTISING AGENCY CHORUS
                 (SFX: Pop music)
                 Think thin.
                 In today's world,
                 To be a success,
                 You must be slim.

MELANEY   I loved that size 8 blue dress.
                 But I could wear it only when I was sick, at size 8.
                 So now I've put my 'old' clothes into the charity bin.
                 And I'm going to be a new 'me' slowly.

BRAIN   At last!
                 She's using me again.
                 I'm so glad to be a working brain.

Discussion Starters

1. What is meant by the term anorexia nervosa?

2. How does it differ from bulimia nervosa?

3. Guilt is a strong emotion in many anorexics. Why do you think this is so?

4. Anorexics are advised to talk the problem over with a friend or member of the family who is willing to listen. Medical help is also advised. What would you do if:
   - A friend was an anorexic and asked for help?
   - You suspected that your sister was suffering from anorexia nervosa?

5. Help for anorexics and bulimics is offered from casualty or outpatients at major public hospitals, community health centres and community mental health centres. What might you say to a friend who needed some help? Would you be prepared to go with a friend to one of these places?

6. You are a television producer responsible for organising a television panel discussion show on controversial subjects. This weeks programme will be on anorexia nervosa.
   - Who will you invite on the panel?
   - What questions will be prepared for the presenter? List at least five.
   - Who could be in the audience?
   - What will you call your programme?

7. You are a reviewer. Write a review of the TV panel show. What worked well? What could be improved? If one of the guests were very thin from anorexia, should the camera avoid close up's or should the filming be realistic? Is it intrusive to focus on a medical problem? Should the guest have the right to request certain editing of the program if it was too personal?

Activities

1. Within the media, there is considerable emphasis on being slim. Music video clips feature slim singers and dancers, models wear tight clothes and commercial 'weight loss' companies show before and after photos of people who have lost kilos.
   - What effect does this have on the average young adult? To what extent is 'being thin' seen as 'being successful'?
   - 'It's impossible to be too thin or too rich.' To what extent would you agree that this is the image projected by the media?
   - Prepare some visuals of recent commercials with unrealistic figures, expectations or messages.

2. Finish the following script. What is the underlying conflict? What will happen next? Show that the two girls are different types of personality by the way they speak and what they speak about.

SARAH	Hi Jane. Haven't seen you for ages. Gosh you've lost a lot of weight.
JANE	Yes.
SARAH	Where have you been hiding yourself?
JANE	Nowhere in particular.

3. Write a weeks worth of entries in the diary of a person suffering from anorexia or bulimia nervosa.

4. You are a journalist researching a feature article on anorexia nervosa for a newspaper. Who might you interview? List the ten questions you would prepare before conducting the interview.

5. Take a song you like and write some new lyrics that touch on the subject of food disorders in some way.

6. Plan a sports fashion parade for a catwalk. The clothes will fit models of all sizes and shapes, work for that sport and all look good. Write the commentary given by the Master of Ceremonies (MC).

The Umbrella Trees with Weak Knees

A conservation spoof

Cast

- Minister for the Trees
- Hangers-on Chorus
- Tall Trees Chorus
- Coach
- Greenies Chorus
- Bushwalkers Chorus
- Workers Chorus
- Bird Chorus
- Sawmill Owner

Props

- Cameras, for Greenies Chorus
- Calculator, for the Sawmill Owner
- Sweat bands and jogging clothes, for the Tall Trees Chorus
- 'Save the Shady Trees' protest banner

- Axes or chainsaws, for the Workers Chorus
- Big boots, sunhats and zinc cream, for the Bushwalkers Chorus

Setting

- Choose your own setting

The Umbrella Trees with Weak Knees Script

MINISTER   Today we will visit the bush.

HANGERS-ON   Yes Minister.

MINISTER   Some of these trees need inspecting.
                         If they are no good, they go.
                         We will cut down the dead wood.

HANGERS-ON   Yes Minister, yes, yes, yes.
                         (Minister for the Trees and Hangers-on chorus exit.)
                         (Tall trees enter and stand together in a line.)
                         (Coach marches up and down inspecting them.)

COACH   Stand straight. Stand tall.
                         Don't slouch.
                         (Crossly) You haven't improved at all.
                         (Tall trees make half-hearted attempts to exercise then give up.)

TALL TREES   We like to give shade,
                         We don't want to fade,
                         We're natural umbrellas
                         For the rosellas
                         But touching our roots,
                         Makes us galahs.
                         (Greenies chorus enters and start taking photographs.)

GREENIES   Trees must grow fit and tall.
                         Let's take photos of you all.
                         To show in papers everywhere.
                         Save the trees. Be aware.

TALL TREES   Yes.

GREENIES   The Minister is coming today.
                         You must look good.
                         Then he'll let you stay.

TALL TREES	Don't make us exercise, please. We're the trees with weak knees. Just let us droop ... Please.
COACH	Exercise is a breeze, Just bend ze knees. *(Bushwalkers chorus come stomping past, wearing big boots, thick socks and floppy sunhats.)*
BUSHWALKERS	We walk ten k every day. Getting fit, the bushy way. What tall trees, They block the sun. Our boots don't hurt. We're having fun. Our hats are shady. Our noses zinc. Don't care how we look. Or what others think.
COACH	Look out for snakes, Near logs and lakes.
BUSHWALKERS	We know that. See! *(They point to their feet.)* Boots and thick socks. Heard the Minister is coming today. We're busy walking, We can't stay.
COACH	*(Demonstrating exercises.)* Make us fit, you said, Or they'll chip chop us dead. You asked me to stay, Getting fit is work, not play.
TALL TREES	*(Bending)* We haven't done this before, Please, Coach, no more! *(Workers chorus enter holding axes or chainsaws and start walking around the trees.)*

WORKERS	Chop. Chop. Chop.
	Chip. Chip. Chip.
	We want to cut down these trees.
	And send woodchips overseas.
	The Minister must listen to us.
	Or we'll make such a fuss.
COACH	*(Shouting)* Touch your knees.
	Lift in the breeze.
TALL TREES	*(Exercising)* But we've got weak knees.
GREENIES	*(Dancing)* Wood chipping shouldn't be done.
	Protesting isn't fun.
	(Bird chorus enter.)
BIRD CHORUS	We don't like to make a fuss,
	But trees are umbrellas for us.
	We need trees.
	Leave them, please.
COACH	My job is to get you fit.
	To make you look great,
	For this inspection trip.
	The Minister for the Trees will decide your fate.
	Hurry up now.
	Or you'll be late.
BIRD CHORUS	*(Looking out)* Here comes the mean anti-greenie.
	Freeze trees.
	(Sawmill Owner enters. Trees freeze.)
SAWMILL OWNER	My sawmill makes wood.
	And the money's very good.
	The workers in the town need me.
	I'm not a mean anti-greenie.
	I just have a job to do.

BIRD CHORUS	*(Flapping around trees.)* Why do you have to sway?
	We like you better the unfit way.
	Our nests go bump,
	Our eggs complain,
	High rise living is such a strain.
SAWMILL OWNER	*(Holding calculator.)* Bip. Bip. Bip.
	Timber or woodchip?
WORKERS	We need the money,
	We need the work.
	Cutting down trees
	Is a job we won't shirk.
	(Minister for the Trees enters followed by Hangers-on chorus.)
MINISTER	Let me see these trees.
	They look weak at the knees.
	Trees try to look fit.
HANGERS-ON	Yes Minister. Yes Minister.
	Yes, yes, yes.
GREENIES	*(Hugging trees.)* You want to cut down shady trees?
	We're against that.
	Totally.
WORKERS	Woodchips aren't the only way,
	New trees can be planted,
	Some shade can stay.
BUSHWALKERS	Our bushwalking is fun.
	But without shade, we'll be burnt by the sun.
	We wear hats.
	We wear cream.
	But that's not enough.
	The noon sun is tough.
	We need shade,
	From these trees.

COACH   I've got an idea.
                 Your trunks are too big for running boots.

TALL TREES   Yes.

COACH   Let's try a roots aerobics class.
                 If the Minister sees you sway,
                 Then he might let you stay.
                 Flex your roots.
                 Wave your shoots.
                 Go. Go. Go.
                 (Trees rap dance to music.)

GREENIES   *(Marching with banner.)* We want to be seen on the TV.
                 Left. Right.
                 Left. Right.
                 Will you be left?
                 Oh, that's all right.

MINISTER   This bush looks pretty fit.
                 What a waste to flatten it.
                 Why don't we plant some more?
                 Well done. Encore.
                 (Minister applauds the trees who are rap dancing.)

Discussion Starters

- Some people are keen to save all trees. What do trees offer us? Why should they be saved? In what circumstances should trees be cut? Does it matter how the wood is used later? Discuss.

- You are a new reporter and your first job is to interview the Minister for the Trees (or the Minister of Environment). What will you ask? Prepare five questions. Where would you like to interview the minister?

- Set up a debate on the topic: 'National forests should be kept at all costs' or 'We need to sell national forest timber to create jobs'.

Activities

1. Clip or scan three to four articles about the environment from this week's magazines or newspapers. What are the main issues being discussed? Prepare a report to share with the rest of the class.

2. A nearby factory pumps waste into the creek and there is an oil slick in your creek. Write a letter of complaint to the manager of the factory, setting out the facts. What else might you do?

3. Write your own script of a conversation between a large gum tree and a blackberry bush. In what way are they different? What might worry them? How might they feel towards tourists? What would be their attitude towards wildlife officers? What might they think of loggers? What could cause an unexpected ending to their conversation?

4. Plan a celebration for 'The Day of the Tree'. Who will be involved? Where will it be held? Any activities like tree climbing? Tree house building? Prepare a competition where people name their top ten trees. Will you include bonsai trees? Heritage trees?

5. Prepare a report on problems with trees in your area. Tree roots can be a problem near some buildings and pipes. Very tall trees may need to be trimmed if they are too close to wires. Who is responsible to pay for the damage caused by a big tree falling in a storm or for other reasons? Check with your council.

6. The SES (State Emergency Service) is called during emergencies. This is a voluntary organisation. Research what kind of training is done by SES workers? What is the youngest age you can volunteer? What kinds of problems do they solve in the community? What equipment or vehicles do they use?

She's Not Here Any More

A script about the death of a classmate

Cast

- Mrs Williams, the teacher
- Class Chorus
- Dale, Kate's friend
- Brian, a classmate
- Kim, a classmate
- Kate's parents

Props

- Flowers – white roses
- Sportsbag, for Kim
- Paper with Brian's poem on it
- Class photographs in an envelope

Setting

- A classroom with desks

She's Not Here Any More Script

(Students enter and sit down, noisily. Brian and Kim fool around with Kim's sportsbag. Mrs Williams, the teacher, enters looking serious and waits for quiet.)

MRS WILLIAMS	Sit down class. I have some bad news to share.
KIM	*(Pushing)* Shut up Brian. Mrs Williams has been crying!
CLASS CHORUS	What's up? What's happened?
MRS WILLIAMS	Kate's mother rang. She wanted me to tell you about Kate.
CLASS CHORUS	She's getting better isn't she?
MRS WILLIAMS	No. I'm afraid that Kate died last night.
CLASS CHORUS	Died? But she's our age!
BRIAN	I've never known anyone who died before.
MRS WILLIAMS	It's okay to feel upset. People show their feelings in different ways. *(Class chorus is upset.)*
MRS WILLIAMS	Some of you might want to walk out of class for a while, then come back when you feel ready to.
BRIAN	Last time I left class, she gave me a detention.
KIM	Shut up Brian. This is real.
CLASS CHORUS	*(Shaking their heads.)* Our insides are turning around. Why did it happen to her? Kate was a popular student. It isn't fair.
MRS WILLIAMS	You knew that Kate had been badly hurt in the accident. But it's still hard to believe that she's dead. I find it hard to understand too.
CLASS CHORUS	We feel numb. We feel sick.

DALE	*(Crying)* Have you got a tissue?
BRIAN	Boys don't cry.
MRS WILLIAMS	Yes they do. We all need to show our feelings.
CLASS CHORUS	We feel nothing. There's a gap inside us.
MRS WILLIAMS	Her parents feel that gap too.
DALE	Everybody will make a fuss about her Mum and Dad. But I was her best friend. Don't my feelings matter too?
BRIAN	Yeah.
KIM	What about the communications project Kate and I were doing? It's due in next week. Now we'll never ... *(Starts to cry.)*
BRIAN	I had a row with her last week.
KIM	*(Crying)* What's different? You're always getting into fights with people.
BRIAN	Yes, but it's too late to make up now.
DALE	Nothing will be the same. I'll never have a friend like her again.
MRS WILLIAMS	The funeral will be tomorrow, Tuesday.
CLASS CHORUS	Funeral!
DALE	That sounds so official. Not like Kate.
MRS WILLIAMS	Some of you may wish to go. If so, I'll make arrangements for you to leave school at the end of second period.
BRIAN	Great! We'll miss French. Er, sorry Mrs Williams.
MRS WILLIAMS	Kate didn't like French either.
DALE	Funerals seem scary. I've never been to one before.

KIM	*(Rummaging in her sportsbag)* I feel guilty that I borrowed her sports gear for the school photos, and didn't give it back.
MRS WILLIAMS	We'll have to clear out Kate's locker. Her parents will want all her things.
KIM	Miss, can't you do that?
MRS WILLIAMS	Yes, I will. Anyone who wants to talk with me privately about Kate can come to my room later. Or you may wish to make something to give to her parents.
DALE	I'd like to make something that would remind us of Kate.
CLASS CHORUS	What?
DALE	I don't know. It was just an idea.
CLASS CHORUS	We could write about the way we feel? Buy her some flowers ... but she wouldn't know.
MRS WILLIAMS	Her parents would.
CLASS CHORUS	And we would.
MRS WILLIAMS	Then who are the flowers for? Us or Kate?
BRIAN	Does it matter?
KIM	Death scares me. Kate hasn't ... hadn't ... finished things. And she's stopped. It's not like on the TV news. We know Kate.
MRS WILLIAMS	The teachers have discussed having a memorial assembly for Kate at school. Perhaps next week.
DALE	You mean a school assembly like Anzac Day?
BRIAN	That was boring.
MRS WILLIAMS	We'd talk about the things Kate has done. And play the music she liked.

KIM	Pop music?
MRS WILLIAMS	Maybe. If that's what she would have liked.
BRIAN	Good thing Kate isn't playing the trumpet. She plays ... played really badly.
KIM	You shouldn't say that now.
BRIAN	Why not? You said yourself she was the worst trumpet player the school ever had. Remember how she got the note wrong at the Anzac assembly that time?
CLASS CHORUS	We remember.
MRS WILLIAMS	It's a custom for friends and relatives to put a notice in the newspaper. Would you like our class to write something special and put it under Kate's name?
CLASS CHORUS	Yes. But what could we write?
MRS WILLIAMS	Anything that shows how you felt about Kate.
KIM	Should we put in some money for the notice? And some flowers?
MRS WILLIAMS	If you like. *(Kim goes around the class collecting money.)*
BRIAN	Dale's crying. Boys don't cry.
MRS WILLIAMS	Yes they do. There's nothing wrong with sharing your feelings. What were her favourite flowers?
KIM	Roses. White roses.
MRS WILLIAMS	*(Opening an envelope.)* Here are the school photos. It doesn't seem the right time to give them out. Here's Kate.
CLASS CHORUS	*(Looking at the photographs.)* We remember her. She's in our heads ... our memories.

MRS WILLIAMS   Now you must settle down class. We have some writing to do. Perhaps you could write about how you feel at the moment?
(Class writes obediently.)

KIM   *(Fiddling with her sportsbag.)*
There's one of Kate's long blonde hairs on my sports gear. She borrowed my track suit last week. It is weird. Like she is telling me something. She's still here, in a way.
(Mrs Williams nods.)

BRIAN   Excuse me Mrs Williams. I wrote this for Kate. Do you think you could give it to her parents or something?

MRS WILLIAMS   That was thoughtful Brian.
(Kate's parents walk through and pick up the paper with Brian's poem on it and start reading.)

KATE'S PARENTS   'For Kate
It's wrong you had to leave so soon,
Our class is different
Now you're not in the room.
We'll remember your trumpet playing,
Though it was off key,
Sorry you're not staying,
We'll miss your company.
You won't miss French,
But we'll miss you,
And the mad things you used to do.
You're still in the class photo,
And we'll keep that too,
But our class is different
Now you're not in the room.'

BRIAN	*(Embarrassed)* It doesn't rhyme and that, but I thought it might help.
KATE'S PARENTS	Thank you Brian. We'd like to read it at Kate's funeral. Or would you read it?
BRIAN	I'm not much good at that sort of thing. *(Class lays flowers and then forms a guard of honour.)*
KATE'S PARENTS	Thank you for coming. We think Kate would have liked that.

Discussion Starters

1. If your friends wished to say goodbye to you using music, which songs would you like them to play? Why those?

2. When my girlfriend died, her mother gave me her watch. Do you think I should wear it?

3. My Grandad always used to play jokes on us. At his funeral, we talked about a funny thing my Grandad did on April Fool's Day. He tried to make us believe there was an elephant on the front lawn. I remembered that so I laughed. But my friends said I was wrong to laugh then because my Grandad was dead. What do you think?

4. A 'euphemism' is a way of avoiding words which make us feel uncomfortable. Because many adults find it hard to say 'dead' or 'death', other words are used to describe the fact that someone has died. Have you heard comments like:
   - "Grandma has gone"
   - "Uncle is far away"
   - "Your baby brother is a star in the sky, you can see him twinkle" ("But what about on cloudy nights? Where is he?")
   - "He's helping God in his garden"
   - "She's sleeping forever" ("Will that happen to me when I go to bed to sleep tonight?")
   - "He's lost his grandmother" ("Was he careless?")
   - "He passed away"

   What is said in your family, if someone dies? How do you feel about using the word 'dead'?

Activities

1. Make a BUT book. This is a fill-the-gap book, as you write how you feel in the space.
   - I feel sad when ...
   - BUT I feel better when ...
   - I feel it is my fault when ...
   - BUT I know it isn't because ...

2. Alex is leaving your school. Make a book for Alex to take. You might include illustrations or photos of:
   - Alex's friends
   - Alex's favourite place to play (under the basketball ring)
   - The classroom
   - His teacher
   - The class photograph
   - Things Alex likes doing (playing basketball, making things in art, playing the drums, mucking around)
   - Things Alex doesn't like doing (picking up papers, spelling tests)
   - Fun things that happened while Alex was here
   - Alex's most embarrassing moment (his pants split)

3. What do you most like doing? If you had only 24 more hours to live, would you:
   - Spend it with friends?
   - Say sorry to some people?
   - Stay with your family?
   - Do something dangerous?
   - Go to sleep?
   - Do something you've always wanted to do?

   Draw five things that you most like doing.

4. Write a letter to yourself at the age you are now. Say what matters most to you NOW. Family? Friends? Pets? Hobbies? Sport? Dreaming? Music? What you most want to do in the future? Date and seal the envelope, put it away safely and open the letter in 20 years time.

The Galactic Gossipmongers

A futuristic look at peer group pressure and highly contagious disease

Cast

- Lani, Zak's ex-girlfriend
- Donna, a student
- Student chorus, who gossip and make ignorant comments
- Coach
- Johnno, a student who actually has VIRO
- Zak, a boy who is thought to have VIRO, a highly contagious intergalactic disease

Props

- Futuristic track suits

Setting

- The Astro-sports changing room at school XYZ in the year 2123. Students are zapping themselves into their track gear

The Galactic Gossipmongers Script

LANI	Any hot goss for us?
DONNA	*(Zapping into her tracksuit)* Heard about Zak?
LANI	Not since the astro-disco last Saturday. What about him?
DONNA	He might have VIRO.
LANI	*(Shocked)* VIRO? How do you know?
DONNA	He's been away having some space tests done.
LANI	That doesn't mean anything! Mum made me have a space test last term when I lost my voice.
STUDENT CHORUS	*(Eavesdropping)* What was wrong with him?
DONNA	Something like astro-fever.
LANI	He's lost a lot of weight. But I thought he was dieting. Like Johnno.
JOHNNO	Yes, I haven't been eating much.
STUDENT CHORUS	Is it catching?
DONNA	What?
STUDENT CHORUS	What you said. VIRO wasn't it?
DONNA	I didn't say Zak has VIRO. He's just having some space tests done.
STUDENT CHORUS	D'you know how you get VIRO?
DONNA	I've heard of a few ways.
STUDENT CHORUS	Like mosquitoes.
LANI	That sounds made up to me. Where did you hear about mosquitoes giving people VIRO?
STUDENT CHORUS	*(Vaguely)* Just around. Everybody knows.

DONNA	I don't know about that. It sounds like an astro-rumour to me.
LANI	Or galactic gossip!
STUDENT CHORUS	And you can catch VIRO from toilet seats.
DONNA	Toilet seats?
STUDENT CHORUS	Or speaking into a public space-phone.
DONNA	I haven't heard that before.
LANI	That's wrong. That's just made up.
STUDENT CHORUS	You can catch VIRO from swimming in a pool, they say.
LANI	Who are "they"?
STUDENT CHORUS	*(Shrugging)* Just the ones who know.
LANI	Can you tell me their names?
STUDENT CHORUS	Not now. Anyway, what about the danger of handling the money Zak touched?
DONNA	What about it?
LANI	Money goes all over the galaxy. Zak isn't the only one to touch it. Anyway he uses a credit card – Galactic Express.
STUDENT CHORUS	Hey, what about the party after the game? Wasn't Zak going to cook the meat on his barbecue? We don't want him touching our astro-bird steaks. We might get VIRO too.
LANI	But you don't know if ... *(Coach enters and interrupts.)*
COACH	Is everybody changed? Where's Zak? We need him to play centre. The Mars Stars team will take some beating.

STUDENT CHORUS	He's not playing in our team.
COACH	Why not?
STUDENT CHORUS	He's having a space-test for VIRO.
COACH	Did he tell you that?
STUDENT	Not exactly … we just heard it. He got it from a Mars mosquito.
COACH	Gossip. Gossip. Gossip. Check your facts before you pass on rumours. Even if Zak did have VIRO, he didn't get it from a Mars mosquito.
STUDENT CHORUS	What d'you mean?
COACH	Catching VIRO from mosquitoes, or toilet seats or phones or swimming pools is nonsense. It doesn't spread like that.
JOHNNO	No, it doesn't.
COACH	It's only passed through blood. That's why we wear gloves for contact sports now.
LANI	Zak and I went to the hydra-pool together last Saturday before we broke up.
JOHNNO	Do you think you might be in danger?
LANI	He cut his finger.
DONNA	Yuk.
LANI	Want a drink, Donna?
DONNA	No thanks. You might have touched it.
LANI	Of course I've touched it.
DONNA	And you're wearing blood red lipstick.
STUDENT CHORUS	You're Zak's girlfriend.
LANI	Ex-girlfriend.

STUDENT CHORUS	There you are. He must have VIRO. That's why you left him. You didn't want him to give it to you.
LANI	No. It's not like that. We had an argument and ...
STUDENT CHORUS	If Zak and Lani both have VIRO ... we'll have to be careful. We might be next.
COACH	Here comes Zak. Give him a fair go. *Zak enters.*
ZAK	Hi. Sorry I'm late for the warm-up.
STUDENT CHORUS	That's okay we know why.
ZAK	You do?
LANI	What did they say?
ZAK	Who?
LANI	The people who gave you the space tests.
ZAK	I'll tell you later.
STUDENT CHORUS	What about us? Don't we have a right to know? We study together ... well ... we study sometimes.
ZAK	We never study together.
JOHNNO	Inter-galactic gossip is the only subject you lot study.
COACH	Hurry up. Stop the gossip. You haven't even got the facts right. Time to start the game. Are you playing Zak?
STUDENT CHORUS	Not in our team. Before he was ... well, okay. He scored lots of star goals. But now ... and Lani is out this week. We don't want her in our team. Anyway, if they have VIRO, they'll have to go to The Place.
ZAK	*(Getting cross)* I'm not taking this ... this gossip. I'm going to fight it.

The Galactic Gossipmongers

COACH	What's the worst thing that can happen?
ZAK	Thinking you have VIRO ... and having to go to The Place.
COACH	Okay. If you have it, that's the worst thing. Plan how you'd cope.
ZAK	I don't know.
COACH	But you will ... cope, I mean and if you can cope with the worst thing, you can cope with the not-so-bad-things that happen.
ZAK	Never thought of it that way before. But it's easy to say if you haven't got VIRO.
COACH	Not yet. But I'm not doing things that would put me at risk.
ZAK	I haven't either. The space tests said I was okay. Just a bit run down.
COACH	That's not what the galactic gossipmongers say. You'll have to face them. And they've already convinced themselves.
LANI	What's wrong Johnno?
JOHNNO	I've got VIRO. The tests came back last week.
COACH	How did you get it?
JOHNNO	From a blood transfusion. Remember when I had that jet-pack accident last term and I crashed into a taxi-jet over the school.
COACH	Yes. I remember.
LANI	But the authorities check on blood now.
JOHNNO	My transfusion was before double-checking day.
ZAK	How are you coping?

JOHNNO	I can cope with feeling sick. But I don't know if I can cope with them! Perhaps I just won't tell them. At first, I couldn't believe it. Then I got cross. Why me? After that I started thinking. If I did lots of exercise and ate healthy foods, maybe it would go away? But that didn't work. I got really fed up. Felt as low as I've ever been. Didn't want to go anywhere or do anything. Nobody seemed to care.
LANI	We care.
JOHNNO	You and who else?
ZAK	What do you want us to do?
JOHNNO	Just treat me the same as usual.
LANI	You mean fight with you?
JOHNNO	That's what used to happen.
COACH	You're following the pattern, you know. Denial. Anger. Bargaining. Depression. And then acceptance.
LANI	Why should we accept what they say?
ZAK	I don't accept it.

Finish the Script

- What do Lani and Zak decide to do?
- How does Johnno cope?
- In the year 2123, what might be "The Place"?
- What is the effect of the galactic gossipmongers?

Activities

You have been asked by a government department to develop a means of conveying the facts about an infectious disease to one of the following groups.
- Children
- Adolescents
- At-risk adults
- A medical audience
- A religious group who claims the infection is a sign of God's displeasure

1. Choose one of these groups. What will be the most effective method to convey the facts to this group? Consider the following possibilities:
    - A commercial for radio
    - A commercial for television
    - A video clip
    - A short documentary
    - A docu-drama
    - YouTube

    Can you think of any other ways?

2. What will be the aim of your production? Will it be to inform, to entertain, to change attitudes, or some other aim? Remember, there's a difference between conveying facts and changing attitudes.

3. Think about the structure of your production. You could use a parody and model your story on one that is well known, for example a nursery story like 'The Three Billy Goats Gruff' or a familiar song like 'Waltzing Matilda' or a famous character like Hamlet (you could begin with his famous 'To be or not to be ...' speech). You might use a narrator, a voice over, a dramatized excerpt or other techniques.

4. In small groups, decide on a title, a cast, the props you will need and the setting. Decide how your script will begin and then write a script. What will be the punchline or twist at the end?

5. Perform your version for the class.

6. Evaluate whether you have conveyed the appropriate facts. Ask the audience what they thought.

Putting It On

A script about haemophilia

Cast

- Class Chorus
- Ben
- Ms Harris, the teacher

Props

- Crutches

Setting

- A classroom

Putting It On Script

(Ben hops past on crutches.)

CLASS CHORUS	Putting it on again Ben?
BEN	No. I'm not.
CLASS CHORUS	Did mummy's little boy have a little fall?
BEN	Yes, I did fall.
CLASS CHORUS	Last week mummy's little boy had his arm in a sling.
MS HARRIS	Stop teasing Ben. Go outside.
CLASS CHORUS	Let's play footy. Are you coming Ben?
BEN	Not today, my knee is sore.
CLASS CHORUS	He's just a sook. Leave him alone. *(Ben hops across to his desk and Ms Harris comes up.)*
MS HARRIS	Ben, Monday next week is an important day. Would you be willing to talk to the class?
BEN	Talk about what?
MS HARRIS	Next Monday is H day.
BEN	Haemophilia Day?
MS HARRIS	That's right.
BEN	They'd just give me a hard time. They always do.
MS HARRIS	You don't have to talk for long. Just tell them how it affects you.
BEN	It will go in one ear and out the other. They never listen to me.

MS HARRIS	On Monday they will. Or they'll get extra homework researching the topic.

(It is now Monday of the following week.)

MS HARRIS	Today Ben is going to talk. It is a special day. It's Haemophilia Day.
CLASS CHORUS	So what?
MS HARRIS	Ben is going to tell you what it means to him.
BEN	Haemophilia is usually hereditary.
CLASS CHORUS	What does that mean?
BEN	You get it from your parents or grandparents. Haemophilia is a blood-clotting disorder. Please Ms Harris. I don't want to do this.
MS HARRIS	Go on Ben. What is the main danger?
BEN	It's not so much getting cut as internal bleeding into the joints.
CLASS CHORUS	Is that why you're such a rotten footballer?
BEN	I have to be careful with contact sports. I must not strain muscles, or get into fights. If a muscle is overworked or I am knocked, I can feel the bleeding start. I have a lot of pain from bleeding into muscles and joints.
CLASS CHORUS	*(Getting interested.)* What do you do then?
BEN	If I bleed, I have to rest the joint and then have treatment.
MS HARRIS	Haemophilia is a chronic bleeding disorder and can't be cured. If the bleeding continues, Ben needs Factor VIII.
CLASS CHORUS	What's that?

BEN	Factor VIII is the blood-clotting factor that is missing from my body.
CLASS CHORUS	Where do you get it from?
BEN	From the Children's Hospital. It's like an infusion.
CLASS CHORUS	What do you get?
BEN	It's human blood plasma that is heat-treated.
CLASS CHORUS	Yuk!
BEN	It's heat-treated to prevent the transmission of AIDS or hepatitis B from the blood donor.
MS HARRIS	There's the bell for recess. Thank you for your talk Ben.
CLASS CHORUS	Want to have a kick of footy Ben? We won't knock you over this time.

Discussion Starters

- What can't a person with haemophilia do?
- What can they do?
- How might a boy with haemophilia create problems for himself?
- How might others create problems for him?
- How might not being able to play contact sports, such as football, affect a boy with haemophilia?
- What sports might be particularly good for haemophiliacs?

Activities

1. Often people suffer from conditions which they prefer not to share with others. Should privacy be respected, or is it better for others in the community to know about the symptoms of the condition, so they may help or be more understanding? Discuss.

2. As well as H Day for Haemophilia Day, what other disabilities could have a special day for consideration of their problems? What is the purpose of having a day to highlight such conditions?

3. Choose either asthma, allergies, epilepsy, arthritis or diabetes and find out three facts about the condition. Present your findings to the class. Do any students in your school suffer from any of these? How do they feel about their condition?

4. At 16 years of age, you can become a blood donor. Usually donors give blood once every three months. It is a voluntary act, you don't get paid. Would you donate blood? Why? Do you know what your blood grouping is? Is it a common or a rare one?

5. People who carry an abnormal gene that may have an effect on their descendants are called 'carriers'. If you were the child of a person with haemophilia and knew you were a carrier, would you decide to have children?

6. With advances in genetic engineering it has become possible to manipulate sets of genes. Imagine that you are the scientist who has made an amazing new breakthrough in connection with Factor VIII. You are holding a press conference. What would you say?

7. You are the organiser of Haemophilia Day at your school. What displays, events and talks will be given? How will you involve everyone?

8. A new student with haemophilia arrives in your class, what would you want to know about them?

9. Prepare a poster competition to share facts about a medical condition, for others of your age. Display the posters on both sides in the school corridor, so it's like an art show. Parents and educators may come to an 'opening'. However, make sure to fact check the posters first with a medical expert.

The House of X

A script about prejudice

Cast

- Mrs Next-door
- Reporter
- Neighbours Chorus
- Dog
- Little Girl
- Mr Noel
- Residents Chorus

Props

- Mrs Next-door's front door
- Fence, for Mr Noel to lean over
- Suitcases, for the Residents to carry

Setting

- A suburban street – the people in the street are outside working in their gardens, cleaning their cars and working on their houses

The House of X Script

(A newspaper reporter is knocking on one of the doors.)

MRS NEXT-DOOR *(Opens the door pushing a reluctant dog in front of her.)* Yes?

REPORTER My name is Amanda Smith. I'm from the Daily News.

MRS NEXT-DOOR Oh. Do you read the news on TV?

REPORTER No. I'm a journalist. I write in the paper.

MRS NEXT-DOOR That's why I don't know your face. *(Dog sniffs the Reporter.)*

REPORTER We've never met before.

MRS NEXT-DOOR Then why are you knocking on my door? You don't want to sell me anything do you? Cosmetics? Dog food? Religion? That's what salespeople usually offer around here.

REPORTER No. I'd like … we'd like a few comments on how you feel about your new neighbours

MRS NEXT-DOOR At 33? Or at 37? The house is empty there.

REPORTER Yes. But it will be used as a special accommodation house and a drop-in centre for people with X. They move in next week.

MRS NEXT-DOOR Over my dead body! I don't want people like that in our street.

REPORTER People like what?

MRS NEXT-DOOR People with X aren't like us.

NEIGHBOURS Lowers the property values. They'll mix with our children. Won't look after the place. People coming and going all night.

REPORTER	I gather that you are not happy about the decision.
MRS NEXT-DOOR	Decision? Who made the decision? We didn't.
REPORTER	The council passed the application last week. You could have complained then.
MRS NEXT-DOOR	I would have complained then, if I'd known.
NEIGHBOURS	We didn't think it mattered. Just another council meeting. But now they're coming to our street! *(Residents chorus enters carrying suitcases.)*
RESIDENTS	We have to live somewhere.
NEIGHBOURS	We think it is a good idea to have a home for these people. But not in our street.
RESIDENTS	We have to live somewhere. Why not in your street?
MRS NEXT-DOOR	We were here first.
LITTLE GIRL	*(Looking up from playing in the street in front of Mrs Next-door's house.)* What is X?
MR NOEL	*(Leaning over the fence.)* The unknown.
MRS NEXT-DOOR	X is something little girls shouldn't worry about.
MR NOEL	People will come to the drop-in centre only during the day for activities. They'll return to their own homes at night. That at least should be okay.
NEIGHBOURS	Parking problems. That's what we'll have next.
MRS NEXT-DOOR	Drivers already cut through our street to miss the main road. We'll have more cars in the street.
MR NOEL	Some of these people will be walking. Or in wheelchairs. Occasionally someone will be in an ambulance or a taxi.
NEIGHBOURS	*(Loudly)* Too much noise in the street.
DOG	Woof. Woof. Woof.

REPORTER	What a nice dog.
DOG	Woof. Woof. Woof.
REPORTER	Does he bark a lot?
MRS NEXT-DOOR	Yes. He's a guard dog. *(Looking afraid, the dog runs inside, when the Little Girl approaches to pat him.)*
LITTLE GIRL	What will the new people be like?
REPORTER	You'll find out soon.
LITTLE GIRL	Will they have any children to play with?
RESIDENTS	No, we don't have any children. But we like them. You can come for afternoon tea if you like.
NEIGHBOURS	She's not allowed to visit you. She might catch something.
RESIDENTS	Friendship?
MRS NEXT-DOOR	We have enough friends. We don't need any more.
REPORTER	*(Mutters)* With a friend like you, who needs enemies?
LITTLE GIRL	I'd like some different friends.
RESIDENTS	We're different.
MRS NEXT-DOOR	How long will they be staying?
REPORTER	How long will you be staying in your house?
MRS NEXT-DOOR	Forever. I've always lived here.
MR NOEL	I moved here a year ago. It takes a while to be accepted.
REPORTER	Are you in favour of the special accommodation house? And the drop in centre?

MR NOEL	Why not? Live and let live. It's nothing to make a big song and dance about.
RESIDENTS	After we've moved in, we thought we might have a street party and invite all the locals.
MRS NEXT-DOOR	Invite us?
RESIDENTS	Would you come?
MRS NEXT-DOOR	I'll think about it.
DOG	*(Coming out from hiding behind Mrs Next-door.)* Woof. Woof. Woof.
RESIDENTS	Don't take too long to think about it. We mightn't be here.
REPORTER	Some people die very quickly, if they have X.

Discussion Starters

What would you do if new people moved in next-door?
- Introduce yourself
- Offer to show them around
- Invite them into your place for a drink or a meal
- Tell them the times of rubbish collections or mail deliveries
- Ask if they needed any help
- Ignore them

Discuss the different reactions among the class.

Would your reaction change in the following situations?
- They did not speak your language
- Their customs were different
- Their animals annoyed you
- They had lots of noisy visitors
- They played loud music in the middle of the night
- Their incinerator smoked into your garden
- They argued loudly
- They dressed or acted differently in some way

Which of the following would you do?
- Talk to them
- Ask how other neighbours felt
- Complain to someone
- Do something else

Activities

1. You want to hold a street party. There has never been one held in your street before. You must contact your local council to get permission to close off the street. Everyone on your street is to be invited but some of the neighbours in your street do not get along with one special household. Discuss how an invitation could be designed that will persuade as many people in the street as possible to come.

2. Parking is a problem in your street on Saturdays because a football match is held nearby and people going to the match often park across driveways. There is an emergency. You need to take a child to hospital. You cannot get the car out of your drive. What will you do? There are many cars parked at the drop-in centre next door because there are many visitors. Yesterday you had a big row with them. You don't feel like asking them for help, but there's little choice. What will you do?

3. You've just arrived home. There is a protest outside your house. People are complaining that you should not be entitled to live in this street. Why are they saying that? What will you say? What will you do?

4. Plan a quirky, colourful but small pottery creature (not a gnome) to 'visit' each house or garden in the street and stay until passed onto another neighbour a week later. This encourages neighbours to laugh and chat with each other. They can take photos too. Be tactful in the type of quirky creature so it doesn't offend any culture. This can also be done with classrooms in a school.

Colours

A colourful approach to prejudice

Cast

- Blue
- Green
- Yellow
- Black
- White
- Red
- MC (Master or Mistress of Ceremonies)
- Protester
- Audience Chorus
- Rainbow Chorus (all the colours together)
- Lighting Engineer, who operates the spotlight

Props

- Each colour wears appropriately coloured clothes
- Blue carries a musical instrument to play 'blues' jazz
- White has a pair of sunglasses

- Spotlight, for Lighting Engineer
- Microphone, for MC
- Protestor carries a sign 'I Protest'

Setting

- Colours are competing in a talent show called the Rainbow Show – the winner will be allowed to perform for special occasions such as weather shows, political events or musical meetings

Colours Script

(The colours introduce themselves to each other as they wait for the MC.)

BLUE I'm Blue.
How do you do? *(Shakes hands with the others.)*

GREEN I'm Green.
I'm easily seen.
On trees, grass and in the bush.

YELLOW Hello, I'm Yellow.
Sunrises are my big scene.

BLACK I'm Black.
You asked me back.

WHITE I'm cool.
I'm White.
Never get uptight.

RED I'm Red.
I'm hot.
Enough said.
(MC comes on to the stage. The audience applauds.)

MC Welcome to the Rainbow Show.
Here we find out which is the most popular colour with the audience.
Each colour will have a turn to perform.
We will start with Blue.

BLUE I'm Blue.
I colour the sky.
But when people say they're Blue,
It means they're cold.
Or sad.
(Plays a sad sound.)

GREEN	Trees and grass are Green. People are called Green, if they are conservationists. *(Paints something green.)*
RED	Some people say, 'Better dead than red.' But I'm not always political.
YELLOW	I'm Yellow I'm the colour of the sun, Or a lemon. *(The lights are turned out.)*
BLACK	Black is beautiful. It is the colour of the unknown. The colour of night. *(A spotlight is turned on White.)*
WHITE	Hi, I'm White. I'm pretty bright. *(Puts on sunglasses.)*
MC	Thank you Colours. Now the audience must judge.
PROTESTOR	*(Stomping across the stage, waving the placard.)* This is all rubbish.
MC	What is?
PROTESTOR	Colours can mean other things.
MC	What sort of things?
PROTESTOR	Some people don't like certain colours. Apartheid means keeping Black and White apart. *(Stands between Black and White.)* Going Red can mean being embarrassed.
GREEN	People who are Green may be seasick.
MC	There are different types of Green, You mean?

PROTESTOR	Of course.
YELLOW	What about me?
PROTESTOR	Being Yellow can mean being cowardly.
YELLOW	But am I popular?
PROTESTOR	Yes. With some people.
MC	What about the 'greenies'? They're popular.
GREEN	One of my lot. We save anything Green.
PROTESTOR	Hey Blue. Do you sing the Blues?
BLUE	Of course. *(Plays musical instrument then sings.)*
BLACK	Hey White. Want to get together?
WHITE	What for?
BLACK	Stripes. Like in a zebra.
WHITE	Been there. Done that. What's new?
BLACK	What's black and white and read all over?
MC	No colourist jokes here please!
BLACK	A newspaper!
MC	*(Ironically)* Thank you Black! Now, who is the most popular?
AUDIENCE CHORUS	We can't choose. We need you all, at different times. Why can't we have a rainbow palette and choose as we need?

RAINBOW CHORUS   We are all popular!

PROTESTOR   You mean job sharing?

LIGHTING ENGINEER
                   No problems.
                   I can put a spotlight on any colour.
                   If you work on the Rainbow, it's not really work.
                   It's only part time, after a rain shower.
                   But I ensure every colour is seen.

Discussion Starters

1. What is your favourite colour? What is the most and the least popular colour in the group? Why? Some names and nicknames are colour based, for example, Red, Sandy, Jade, Amber. Are there any 'colour' names in your group of friends?

2. Colours are often associated with moods. For example, blue is associated with feeling sad and red with anger or embarrassment. List some of the other associations with particular colours.

3. Colour prejudice is often based on skin colour. What difference would it make in your world if your skin were a different colour? Brown? White? Yellow? Purple?

4. Discrimination means to treat a person or persons differently because of a certain category such as race, age, or sex. Discuss

Activities

1. Edward de Bono, the lateral thinker, proposes a six hats approach to solving problems. He suggests that you should figuratively put on a particular coloured hat, and seek a new a way of thinking, to solve a problem. White hat means thinking like a computer – rationally and with no emotion. Black hat means thinking of all the negative aspects. Yellow hat is all the positive, optimistic, 'sunny' ways of thinking. Red hat is the emotive 'gut' reactions. Green hat is brainstorming in a productive way. Blue hat is the organising and co-ordinating type of thinking to gather all the bits together.

   Choose a problem and try the 6 hats approach to solving it.
   - In groups of six, each imagine that you are wearing a different coloured 'hat' and approach the problem from that angle
   - Each person could then try each 'hat' in turn

2. Colour palettes: Plan the contrasting colours which you will use to design a cover for a book. Readers need to be able to pick out the title against the background. Those who are colour blind have

trouble distinguishing certain colours or tones. Graphic designers often use a colour palette online with opposite sectors on a wheel to check on the best contrasting colours. Share the best cover you have found with contrasting colours. Share the worst too.

3. Research your local supermarket. In what ways are colours in the setting and on products used to entice you to buy more? HINT – Green is often considered calming.

4. Prepare a 3 course meal which is only one colour. HINT – Blue is the most difficult. It's important to note that health wise, it's better to have a range of colours and nutrients in your food.

The Bunga-Berry Pavlova Dream with Whipped Cream

A melodrama about a country town initiative to attract tourists

Cast

- Mayor
- Reporter
- Horrible Horace 'The Baddie'
- Olaf the Offsider, who works for Horrible Horace
- Hens, any number
- Bad Hen, who lays bad eggs and works for Horrible Horace
- CWA (Country Women's Association) chicks with attitude who cook awesome sponges
- Cows, any number
- Sulky Cow, who gives sour cream and works for Horrible Horace
- Pavlova Pat, 'The Goodie', who is trying to make the perfect pavlova
- Primary aged children, any number, who cook gingerbread people
- Judges, any number
- RSL (Returned and Services League of Australia) drop scone cooks, any number
- Non-speaking parts – they act or mime, e.g. extra cooks

Props

- 'Back to Bunga' sign
- Pavlovas. These could be made out of plaster. Several needed on a table labelled Try No 1, Try No 2 and so on
- Sandwich Board which says 'Eat Horrible Horace's Pies, You'll Never Get Better!'
- Clock
- 4 bad eggs
- 4 big eggs
- CWA sponges
- Gingerbread people
- RSL drop scones
- Horrible pie
- Pavlova with berries

Setting

- A small country town called Bunga, during 'Back to Bunga' week – there is a 'Back to Bunga' sign on the wall

The Bunga-Berry Pavlova Dream with Whipped Cream Script

MAYOR Good evening.
(Looks at watch.)
Only 24 hours to go.
Only 24 hours before the winner is announced.

REPORTER What winner?

MAYOR The winner of the 'Back to Bunga' food competition, of course. This is our 'Back to Bunga' week of celebrations.

REPORTER What is the food competition?

MAYOR Haven't you heard? Bunga is going to be the biggest tourist attraction in the country. I am the Mayor of Bunga. I have offered a prize for the best plate of food Bunga cooks can make. But there is one rule.

REPORTER What's that?

MAYOR The food must be made from Bunga ingredients, and it must be on the table at the town hall by 9am tomorrow morning.

REPORTER What's the prize?

MAYOR That's a secret.
(Horrible Horace and Olaf walk on stage, but the Mayor doesn't notice. Horrible Horace wears a sandwich board which says 'Eat Horrible Horace's Pies, You'll Never Get Better.')

HORRIBLE HORACE It's not a secret to me. I am Horrible Horace. This is Olaf, my offsider. I own the Horrible Pie Company. And I'm going to win the prize.

OLAF What is it?

HORRIBLE HORACE	A contract to feed all the tourists who visit Bunga. I will charge them what I like. The prize is worth millions.
MAYOR	All over Bunga, they are cooking tonight. Sponges. Drop scones. Pavlovas. *(He leaves the stage. Reporter moves to one side and watches. Now and then he takes notes.)*
HORRIBLE HORACE	Pavlovas! Pavlova Pat is making a special pavlova. I must stop Pat. Come on Olaf. *(They leave, then hens bustle across stage.)*
HENS	Cluck, Cluck, Cluck. Tonight they all want eggs. Eggs for sponges. Eggs for drop scones. Eggs for pavlovas. *(CWA ladies come on stage and shoo hens away. Horrible Horace comes back.)*
CWA LADIES	Hurry up. Hurry up. We need more eggs. We can't make sponges without eggs.
HORRIBLE HORACE	Why not? I make my meat pies without meat. *(Cows wander on and CWA Ladies leave.)*
COWS	Moo. Moo. Moo. Tonight they all want cream. Cream for sponges. Cream for butterfly cakes. Cream for pavlovas.
ALL	Pavlovas! *(Pavlova Pat drags table on stage. The pavlovas are labelled Try No 1, Try No 2 and so on.)*
PAVLOVA PAT	If at first you don't succeed ...
HORRIBLE HORACE	Cheat!
PAVLOVA PAT	*(Doesn't hear.)* If at first you don't succeed, try, try again ... *(Looks up at clock.)* After midnight, I'll have one more try.

(Puts hand in egg bowl.)
No more eggs. What will I do? I must win the prize. I have nothing else left. My pavlova shop was burnt down by Horrible Horace. He wants people to buy his pies, but they like my pavlovas better.
(Hens march across the stage.)

HENS No more eggs. We're on strike. We're sick of laying around. We want better bird conditions. No more eggs tonight.

PAVLOVA PAT Please. Just four more eggs. I only need four more eggs.

HENS Horrible Horace warned us about you. Four eggs tonight and tomorrow you'll want four thousand. No more eggs. No more eggs-ploitation.

PAVLOVA PAT Sounds like a 'Horrible' joke. I knew he was behind this. But I can't make pavlovas without eggs.

HENS He makes meat pies without meat.

PAVLOVA PAT Greasy, fatty pies. Horrible pasties. Unsausage rolls. And unchicken rolls. Yuk!

BAD HEN I will help you. Have four of my eggs.
(Horrible Horace is laughing in the background.)

PAVLOVA PAT *(Smells eggs.)*
No thanks.

BAD HEN Horrible Horace told me to…

PAVLOVA PAT He's a bad egg too.

HENS NO more eggs tonight. Strike. Strike. Strike …
(Hens bustle away.)

PAVLOVA PAT I must do something. Where can I get some eggs.
(Thinks)
I know!

(*Pavlova Pat runs off and returns with four large eggs. Olaf moves into the background. Whispers to Horrible Horace and starts taking notes. Horrible Horace leaves.*)

PAVLOVA PAT   Ordinary pavlovas are sugar, egg white, cream and passion fruit. My pav is different.
It doesn't have passion fruit on top.
It doesn't have kiwi fruit on top.
It doesn't have bananas on top.
It has Bunga fruit.
This the one and only Bunga-berry Pavlova Dream with Whipped Cream …
Eureka! I have found it … the perfect pav.
(*Pat reaches for the cream.*)
Oh no! The last of the cream. I bet the cows are on strike too.

COWS   Moo. Moo. Moo. We're on strike too. No more milk. No more yoghurt. No more cream. No more butter.

PAVLOVA PAT   Did Horrible Horace tell you to do this?
(*Cows nod.*)
Why?

COWS   He promised to put carpet squares in our cow yard. And satellite movies during milking.
(*Olaf shakes his head disbelievingly.*)

OLAF   Silly cows.
(*Sulky Cow comes forward.*)

SULKY COW   I'm Sulky Cow. I'll help. Have some of my cream.

PAVLOVA PAT   (*Tastes*)
It's sour.

SULKY COW   Of course. It goes with my personality.
(*Pavlova Pat gets an idea and takes the sour cream.*)

PAVLOVA PAT	Thanks Sulky Cow. Horrible Horace didn't really mean for you to help me, but you have. *(Pavlova Pat leaves with his pavlovas. Cows wander away. Mayor arrives and throws cloth across table.)*
MAYOR	Good morning. Nearly 9 o'clock. The judges are ready. Here come the Bunga cooks. *(All the cooks arrive carrying their plates. Judges follow.)* Number 1. The CWA sponge. *(CWA Ladies bow.)* Number 2. Primary school students' gingerbread men ... er people. *(Students bow.)* Number 3. RSL drop scones. *(RSL cooks bow.)* Number 4. Horrible Horace's pie. *(Horrible Horace scowls.)* *(Audience boo.)* Number 5. The Bunga-berry Pavlova Dream with Whipped Cream *(Pavlova Pat bows.)* *(Judges taste all the food including the pie.)*
JUDGES	Yuk. *(Then Judges taste the pavlova.)* Unusual. Sweet and Sour pavlova. Bunga-berries. A local recipe. How clever. This is the winner.
HORRIBLE HORACE	No. Pat can't be the winner. Those eggs weren't laid in Bunga. The winner had to use Bunga ingredients.
JUDGES	Is this true? Where were the eggs laid?
PAVLOVA PAT	In Bunga.
HORRIBLE HORACE	But I told the hens to go on strike!

MAYOR	Did you? Then I can blame you Horrible Horace. I missed my boiled egg at breakfast this morning. That was your fault.
PAVLOVA PAT	My eggs were laid in Bunga but not by a hen. They are duck eggs.
MAYOR	Duck eggs? No rule against that I suppose.
HORRIBLE HORACE	What about the sour cream? Sulky Cow gave you sour cream.
JUDGES	No rule against that.
MAYOR	Then Pavlova Pat is the winner. Here is your contract. A lifetime supply of pavlovas for all tourists who visit Bunga. I will pay the bill ... or the council will.
PAVLOVA PAT	Thank you very much Mr Mayor. Now I will be able to cook pavlovas every day.
REPORTER	Our newspaper is looking for unusual recipes for a special cookery book. Perhaps ... ?
PAVLOVA PAT	Perhaps ... Let's eat this one first. *(All sit down to eat.)*
MAYOR	Tastes different from my usual breakfast. Tourists will love it. Our greatest attraction.
ALL	The Bunga-berry Pavlova Dream with Whipped SOUR Cream.

Discussion Starters

1. Does your area have any food named after it or associated with it? E.g. Tasmania's Tamar Valley yoghurt? Goulburn Valley fruit? Find five places which are linked with special recipes or types of food.

2. The Great Vanilla Slice Triumph began in Ouyen in 1998. After that Victorian premier Jeff Kennett claimed the vanilla slice from the town's Mallee Bakery was the best he'd ever tasted. Over the years the competition attracted entries from interstate. In 2012 it moved to Merbein. For three years it was held in Mildura but then returned to Merbein for the 2022 Triumph.
Discuss in small groups. If you were an event organiser given the task of attracting people to your area, which food or local produce might you feature? How might you organise a tour of the orchard, farm or factory? E.g Lavender farm with lavender scones to eat, but also perfumes and pillows?

3. Silo art has drawn many tourists to certain country towns in recent years. How would you organise a mural in your town, which is NOT graffiti. Discuss.

Activities

1. Often towns have a 'Back To ...' celebration. You are the manager for your school's 'Back To ...' event.
   - Organise a lunch?
   - A parade?
   - Photo display?
   - Famous ex-students to visit?
   - Bush band?
   - Differences between then and now?
   - Will people dress up in old style clothing?

2. You've probably heard of a wine tasting where judges have to select the best wine from unlabelled bottles. A berry tasting is a little different.

- Blindfold the judge
- Place several kinds of berries on a plate – strawberry, blackberry, loganberry etc
- Allow the judge to feel and taste each berry
- Count how many the judge gets right
- Try making your own pavlova
- Mock up a cooking program and record it in your favourite medium of multi-media

3. Research and prepare a 3-minute talk on 'How did the sweet get its name?' or 'Who was Pavlova?'. You may find there are several interpretations of who should get the credit for the sweet.

The Parts of Speech TV Show

A script about finding the right words in difficult situations

Cast

- Host – charming, but not quick-witted
- Parts of Speech (each labelled on t-shirt or a sign)
    - Noun, naming word
    - Verb, doing word
    - Adjective (who shadows/follows Noun)
    - Adverb (who follows Verb)
    - Pronoun (instead of a Noun)
    - Conjunction (which joins)
- Punctuation team (optional extras, shaped like their names)
    - Apostrophe
    - Commas
    - Full Stop
    - Question Mark
    - Exclamation Mark
- Audience (any number, who participate by voting, buzzing or other actions)

- Judges (2) who have to decide which parts of speech are the most important

Props

- Cardholders (actors) for question words
  - Who?
  - Why?
  - How?
- T-shirts or signs for Parts of Speech
- Voting cards and pens for audience, so they can tick their favourite
- Sticky labels, for audience to put on actors playing parts of speech
- Microphone for host
- TV camera for operator (optional)
- Buzzers for audience votes
- SFX (Pre-recorded)
  - 2 x 30 second TV commercials which can have dancing/singing or topical satire. Or they can link to the parts of speech.
  - TV show introductory music

Setting

- TV studio with audience

The Parts of Speech TV Show Script

	(*Who? Why? How? sign holders in a line to the side of Host with microphone.*)
SFX	*TV INTRO MUSIC*
HOST	Welcome. I am your TV host. This is the top rating Parts of Speech Show. Tonight, we have two judges. Parts must convince us that one of them is the most important in a sentence. Our studio audience will help. Tell the audience about their buzzers, Chris.
CHRIS	Test your buzzer please. (*Audience hit buzzers.*)
HOST	You help the judges decide. (*Sign holders lift their cards. Host points to each as holder shouts the information.*)
WHO	Who are you?
WHY	Why do you matter?
HOW	How can you be used?
HOST	Thank you sign holders. Each Part of Speech has only one minute in which to answer as many of these questions as possible.
CHRIS	This is a show about choice. So we offer different ways to vote or help the judges.
HOST	You have a buzzer and under your seats are voting cards. (*Members of the audience squirm to find them.*) Take notes as the Part speaks. (*Audience check cards.*)

HOST	We'll be back after the break, ready to hit those buzzers FOR Parts of Speech!
SFX	*FAST PACED 30 SECOND TV SONG & DANCE COMMERCIAL*
HOST	Let's welcome our first contestant. What part do you play?
VERB	I'm a Verb. I do things. I'm an action kind of guy/girl. *(Appeals to audience to act.)* Jump. Stretch. Clap. *(Audience do the actions.)*
HOST	Buzz if you think verbs matter.
SFX	*AUDIENCE BUZZ* *(Judges nod and make notes.)*
CHRIS	Buzz is a verb too. Here are some stick-on labels. Write your favourite verb ... and stick it on our Verb.
AUDIENCE	What about Kick?
VERB	Kick is an action. But there are better verbs. Just stick them on me. I'll run around now and collect a few from the audience.
CHRIS	*(Sticks label on Verb)* Here. I wrote vote as a verb. I vote for you. *(Adverb clutches Verb.)*

ADVERB	I'm an adverb I add to the verb. That's why I'm following Verb Jump ... slowly ... I'm slowly ...
HOST	*(Whispers to Chris.)* Is 'think' a verb?
CHRIS	Yes. It's a doing word.
HOST	I don't think much.
CHRIS	You think slowly. Slowly is the adverb. *(Adverb gives a thumbs up.)* *(Audience clap. Verb followed by Adverb collects stick-on votes jogging around and Contestant 2 Noun comes out as judges chat.)*
HOST	Good evening. Who are you?
JUDGES	*(Mutter)* Can't the Host read her label?
NOUN	I'm a Noun. I'm the name of something. Like Studio. Or Host.
HOST	That's my name. *(Alarmed)* There's someone following you. Are you being stalked? *(Noun looks around quickly.)*
NOUN	Just an Adjective. They're always following us Nouns. *(Sign holders lift their cards. Host points to each as holder shouts the information.)*
WHO	Who are you?
WHY	Why do you matter?
HOW	How can you be used?
HOST	Thank you sign holders.

The Parts of Speech TV Show

ADJECTIVE	*(Following Noun closely.)* I'm an Adjective. I add news to the Noun. That's why I keep close. Like if the Noun is studio I'm cool to go in front of studio. This is a cool studio.
HOST	*(Shivering)* Yes it is cool in here.
JUDGES	It is also a small, noisy, dark, smelly studio. Small and noisy are also adjectives. *(Adjective gives a thumbs up.)*
ADJECTIVE	Hey Noun, I make your life more meaningful.
NOUN	*(Pushes away.)* You're just an extra.
ADJECTIVE	But I add colour and emotion to spice up your life.
NOUN	I'm just a name like, the word for house.
ADJECTIVE	I'm the renovated house or the expensive house, or the designer house. I make your life more meaningful.
NOUN	… or the dog house …
ADJECTIVE	*(Annoyed)* Maybe. I could be the dog part of your house, but … 'dog' on its own is just a noun, the name of something.
HOST	Man's best friend.
ADJECTIVE	I'm the best part of best friend.
AUDIENCE	*BUZZ* *(Preposition and Conjunction creep in.)*
HOST	Who are you?

PREPOSITION	I'm a Preposition. A sort of at, in, out kind of guy. I get followed by nouns and pronouns. They're always following me up hills, down stairs, behind doors ... Hey audience, want to vote for me? Stick up for me?
AUDIENCE	*BUZZ*
CONJUNCTION	I'm a Conjunction. I'm a joiner, great at linking people. Parts of Speech need me to link them. That's my job. Otherwise they'd be all over the place. *(Moves the parts into a line.)* Are all the parts of a sentence here? Get in line. Make a sentence.
CHRIS	Anyone missing?
QUESTION MARK	*(Runs on to end of sentence.)* Sorry I'm late. I'm a Question Mark. This sentence is a question, isn't it?
AUDIENCE	*(Nodding)* Yes.
CHRIS	Maybe the audience can form their bodies into a question mark shape? Try? *(Audience shape themselves like a question mark.)*
QUESTION MARK	*(Admiringly)* Great shape! *(Pronoun pushes Noun out of the line.)*
HOST	Who are you?
PRONOUN	I'm a Pronoun. I can stand in for a noun in a sentence. I'm like he or she or it, or even they ...
CHRIS	Just a stand-in, like in the movies?

PRONOUN	An important stand in. I stop boring, boring, boring repetition. *(Remaining parts rush on stage.)*
REMAINING PARTS	You forgot us.
APOSTROPHE	*(Pushes in line and jumps around in protest.)* Hey!
CHRIS	We've had a late request for the Apostrophe because most people don't know where she should go … in front, behind the s or … just perch on the top …
APOSTROPHE	I'm an Apostrophe. I know where I should go, But most people forget me, or they can't spell my name. A.P.O.S.T.R.O.P.H.E. That's me.
EXCLAMATION MARK	I'm an exclamation mark. I draw attention to something special. But I'm over exposed. People use me too often.
CHRIS	Let's move.
SFX	*THE TUNE OF HOKEY POKEY* *(Audience encouraged to follow dance-fit actions.)* You put a comma here, You put a full stop there A question there and you turn it all around. You do the sentence fit And you turn around That's what it's all about!
HOST	Time has run out. Thank you Parts of Speech Judges and audience must now decide.

	From those presented, who is to be our most important part of speech tonight? Fill in your voting cards now.
CHRIS	Ready? I'll collect the cards. *(Allow audience time to fill in the cards. Then Chris adds them up quickly. Judges chat.)*
HOST	We'll be back after the break, with the judges' report.
SFX	*FAST PACED 30 SECOND TV SONG & DANCE COMMERCIAL*
HOST	Form a line. Make a sentence. Then we'll ask the judges. *(Opens envelope.)* The judges have decided that all parts of speech matter equally. It's a tie. The prize goes to the whole sentence. Take a bow. *(All bow.)*
CHRIS	Tomorrow night, we will be talking about the contributions of THE PUNCTUATION TEAM! *(All tumble onto stage.)* Full Stop! Commas Question Marks And Exclamation Marks!
SFX	*TV SHOW MUSIC FADING OUT*
QUESTION MARK	What is the prize?
HOST	You come back as a judge?

Discussion Starters

1. Prepare a fast survey. What is the most frequently used word by each student in the class? Are there any used by more than one student? 'Like' is an over-used word but it's often a space filler while the speaker tries to think of an answer. Others use 'Um' as a space filler. Swear words are often space-fillers too, or show the person has a limited vocabulary. Youthful language changes fashion quickly, often compliments or insults.
   - What is the fashionable, complimentary term? e.g. 'Cool' is out of date
   - What is the negative or put down term? (No swearing). E.g. 'gross' is out of date
   - Where do the new words come from? Media? Shortened versions of other words? Initials?
   - Why do people use them? To show they are part of the 'in' group? To shock?

2. Prepare 5 words to share which are brands but became 'generic' words internationally. E.g. Biro, Bandaid, Kleenex, Escalator, Googling, Xerox, Bubblewrap, Frisbee, Jetski. Discuss if there are any local school words/names for places, uniforms or objects that most students know but which are not written down yet.

Activities

1. Plan an event called Eat Your Words. Invite students to bring food to share which has a link to parts of speech or punctuation. E.g. Nouns iced on cake, commas on cupcakes, alphabet soup, question mark biscuits etc.
   Are there any 'Australianisms' which newcomers find difficult to understand at first? Any funny incidents? E.g. Custom of being asked to 'bring a plate' (meaning WITH food on it to share.)

2. Write, as a group, a TV gameshow quiz modelled on this script but choose a different theme for the cast.
For example you could have virtues and vices (or good and bad) teams competing. In medieval morality plays and folk drama, they believed in seven vices which acted. In the morality play, vices were types of evil or deadly sins and tempted the everyday man towards his downfall. Pride, envy, wrath, avarice, sloth, gluttony, and lust were the sins. Because the audience were illiterate, the storytelling was oral and acted as a religious commercial to 'be good'. Later these vices and virtues had updated names like lazy for sloth or anger for wrath. Medieval virtues included chastity, temperance, charity, diligence, patience, kindness, and humility which were later updated.
If you are dealing with 'abstractions' like 'gluttony' (greed) you need something for the actor to do on stage. So, a singing or dancing chorus is useful and the framework of a quiz show helps.

3. Prepare 5 questions to ask if you were the host/ess of a sequel to 'The Parts of Speech TV Show'.

4. Prepare some simple costumes for your cast. You may suggest all wearing black tights and tops with just a name or a sign on their chest. Masks are another option.

Sleuth Astrid: The Mind Reading Chook

A simple satire with complex ideas for gifted students

Script adapted from Hazel Edwards' eBook series *Sleuth Astrid: The Mind Reading Chook*, illustrated by Jane Connory.

Cast

- Narrator, can have giant 'prompt' book
- Astrid, a chook sleuth with a mobile under one wing, who pecks on a laptop and microphone. Carries ID card
- Merlin the Magician with cloak and stick
- Flopsy, a bad tempered white rabbit in magic act
- Boy from audience
- Audience (any number) who clap and mime, but don't have lines to speak
- Ben, the agent
- Keeper of Lost Property
- Rooster who laughs at own jokes
- Hens (any number)
- Chicks Chorus (any number) including Inspector Clues, the French chick

- Security Guard at shopping centre
- Guard dog on leash
- Perfume shop girl
- Optional non-speaking parts:
  - Aunty Rhoda as a Hot Chicken Shop Special Sandwich with lettuce, mustard and pickles
  - Uncle as a Feather Bed Shop chicken feathers

Props

- Microphone for Astrid to peck answers.
- Mobile.
- Car with big label 'Merlin the Marvellous'
- 3 bottles of perfume/after-shave named Forget, Stop, Remember
- Giant pack of cards for tricks
- Lost property, e.g. umbrellas, shoes etc
- Motorcycle (Harley Davidson) with EGGS-PERT numberplate
- ID card for Astrid
- Photo of Merlin
- SFX: Music to start Magic Show and rings for mobile phone

Setting

- Shopping centre magic show

Sleuth Astrid: The Mind Reading Chook Script

SFX	*MAGIC SHOW MUSIC*
NARRATOR	This is the Magic Show.
MERLIN	*(Bows)* I'm Merlin the Magician. I do magic tricks.
AUDIENCE	*(Clap)*
ASTRID	*(Bows and mobile gets in the way.)* My name's Astrid. I'm a Mind Reading Chook.
AUDIENCE	*(Clap)* *(Chicks Chorus parade, showing off.)*
CHICKS CHORUS	We're chicks. You're just a chook.
ASTRID	Chickens are ordinary, but I'm special.
NARRATOR	It's time for a magic trick. Merlin will need a helper from the audience. *(Audience react. Some want to help, others try to hide.)*
MERLIN	I'd like that boy in the front row to come out to help me.
BOY	Me?
MERLIN	Yes. You. Come and pick a card from this pack.
NARRATOR	Merlin will shuffle the cards. The boy must pick one.
BOY	This one.

MERLIN	*(Holds card up high.)* Reading is an important skill. This is my famous mind-reading chook. Astrid will tell us the card. Keep it covered. She will read it from the back! *(Swirls cape and waves stick.)*
NARRATOR	See the microphone in front of Astrid. Astrid has to peck her answers. Yes is one peck. No is two pecks.
MERLIN	Astrid, is it a red card?
ASTRID	*(Pecks once.)*
MERLIN	Astrid is right. It is a red card.
AUDIENCE	*(Clap)*
MERLIN	Astrid, is it a picture card?
ASTRID	*(Pecks once.)*
MERLIN	Astrid is right. It is a picture card.
AUDIENCE	*(Clap harder.)*
NARRATOR	This is amazing. Can this chook read? She will peck once for yes and twice for no.
ASTRID	*(Talks directly to the audience as others freeze.)* It's a red King of Hearts. I'm supposed to peck the right card. That's easy for me. I'm the star. And Merlin gives me clues in the questions.
SFX	*(Mobile rings.)* RING RING
NARRATOR	Astrid has other part-time jobs. She's an actor and she solves mysteries.
ASTRID	*(Looks at screen.)* Hello Ben. Got a job for me?

BEN	It's a TV commercial. They want you to act as a chicken. Should be easy.
ASTRID	Too easy. Who's it for?
BEN	The Hot Chicken Shop.
ASTRID	No way. I haven't forgotten what happened to Aunty Rhoda.
NARRATOR	There was a mystery about what happened to Aunty Rhoda in the Hot Chicken Shop. Astrid found out that Aunty Rhoda became a Special Sandwich with lettuce, mustard and pickles.
ASTRID	I won't even go near that shop now. And I won't act in Feather Bed Shop commercials either.
BEN	Why not?
ASTRID	My poor Uncle is just feathers at the Feather Bed Shop now. What sort of agent are you?
BEN	Ok. I've got a different job for you.
ASTRID	What is the job?
BEN	It's Merlin. He's lost something he needs for his 3 o'clock Magic Show.
ASTRID	*(Hopefully)* Has he lost Flopsy?
NARRATOR	Flopsy is Merlin's white rabbit. She has long ears and a bad temper and thinks she's the star.
BEN	No.
ASTRID	Has he lost his contact lens again?
BEN	No. This time he has lost his sense of humour. He can't laugh or smile any more. Nothing is funny for him.

ASTRID	When did he lose it?
BEN	Before he got up this morning.
ASTRID	Does he know where he lost it?
BEN	No. That's why you've got the job of finding it. Before 3 o'clock.
ASTRID	What about my fee?
BEN	Do you want the usual?
ASTRID	Yes please. I'd like the latest 'Find the Egg' game.
NARRATOR	Most agents are paid 10% of what their clients earn. But Astrid is a hi-tech hen who likes to be paid in new computer games like 'Eggs Galore' or 'Find the Egg'. So Ben gets to play a few games.
BEN	Goodbye. *(Others 'unfreeze' as Astrid turns off phone.)*
MERLIN	*(Swishes cane.)* Nothing is funny. I feel grumpy all the time. *(Cane breaks.)* Oh no! Everything is going wrong. Last night I forgot where I parked my car, so I had to catch the train home. *(Merlin tries to glue cane together and it sticks to his fingers.)* I'm stuck!
FLOPSY	*(Bounds on.)* Find the car first. I don't want to walk to work at the Magic Show. Come on.
ASTRID	Get lost Flopsy!
NARRATOR	Astrid pecks around trying to find where Merlin lost things.

ASTRID	If you want to find something, check the last place he went. *(Checks carpark and finds a car with big label 'Merlin the Marvellous.')* Found the car. Now the sense of humour. Where could he have left that?
NARRATOR	*(To audience.)* Where would you look for a lost sense of humour? Joke book? In the principal's office? Magic shop with tricks? Astrid tried all those. Then she rang Merlin.
SFX	*RING RING RING*
ASTRID	Hello Merlin. Happy about getting your car back?
MERLIN	I don't feel like laughing. But thanks for finding my car.
ASTRID	Now I'm on the case of your missing sense of humour.
NARRATOR	Merlin used to play jokes. He used to laugh too. Where did he lose his sense of humour? Astrid the mind reading sleuth will find it.
ASTRID	You start where the lost thing was last seen. Where did Merlin laugh the last time? He caught the train home last night. Maybe he left it on the train? I'll try Railway Lost Property?
NARRATOR	The Keeper of Railway Lost Property is in charge of everything that is lost on trains
KEEPER	This is Railway Lost Property. I'm in charge here. I'm the Keeper. We have thousands of umbrellas. Lots of shoes and sports gear. And some VERY unusual objects. *(Shows example.)*
ASTRID	Do you have a sense of humour?

KEEPER	Of course I have one. It's mine. Need it in this job.
ASTRID	No, I mean a 'lost' sense of humour. Merlin the Magician has lost his. I'm looking for lost laughs and jokes.
KEEPER	Well, it hasn't been handed in here. When did he lose it?
ASTRID	Yesterday.
KEEPER	When does he need it back?
ASTRID	Before the 3 o'clock Magic Show. He must laugh and joke in his work.
NARRATOR	Astrid decided to check out the farmyard. It is the gossip centre. The hens know everything. *(Chicks chorus, hens and the rooster peck across the farmyard.)*
ASTRID	Have you heard anything funny?
CHICKS	We might have.
HENS	Maybe.
ASTRID	Merlin the Magician has lost his sense of humour. I must find it before his 3 o'clock magic show.
ROOSTER	*(Sneering)* So you're the hard boiled detective. Hard boiled…get it? *(Laughs at own joke.)*
INSPECTOR CLUES	Rooster fell off the henhouse roof yesterday. Merlin was here and he laughed. So Merlin must still have had it then.
ASTRID	That's a clue.
INSPECTOR CLUES	Would you like my help with this case?
ASTRID	No thanks. Unless it's a French mystery where you have to speak French, I can manage.

ROOSTER	If you want to know anything, ask me. Not the chick.
NARRATOR	Rooster thinks he's top of the pecking order. His job is to look after his hens. But he's always telling BAD jokes, and then laughing.
ASTRID	Heard any laughs around here? Smiles?
ROOSTER	Why? Is laughing at my jokes a crime? *(Laughs so loudly he falls beak first into water bowl.)*
HENS	*(Giggle and then laugh.)* *(Rooster shakes himself and stalks off.)*
NARRATOR	In between jobs, Astrid stays in her loft above the bird yard. All kinds of birds rent space. Ducks. Geese. Even a swan who teaches ballet. Astrid can park her motor cycle alongside. Not many chooks ride Harleys. Astrid pecks on her laptop.
ASTRID	*(Typing)* Going to leave a question on Chooks Anonymous. Others read it and leave answers. "Lost. Sense of humour belonging to Merlin. Please contact Astrid the Mind Reading Chook." Hope someone leaves me a clue before 3 o'clock. Might play a few games … *(Types)* Now I'll check my messages. Oh no. I typed Cook instead of Chook. How embarrassing!
SFX	*RING RING RING*
ASTRID	Astrid speaking.
SECURITY GUARD	Are you the chook looking for a laugh?
ASTRID	I'm Astrid, the part-time sleuth. My client has lost his sense of humour. Have you heard a lost laugh?
SECURITY GUARD	Yes.
ASTRID	How do you know it belongs to Merlin?

SECURITY GUARD	He was here at our shopping centre last night.
ASTRID	Which shopping centre?
SECURITY GUARD	Aren't you supposed to read minds?
NARRATOR	There are millions of shopping centres.
ASTRID	I need a few clues. Even a mind reader can't get it right every time.
SECURITY GUARD	I'm the security guard at Central Carpark. I patrol with my dog.
ASTRID	How big is your dog? I want to keep my last tail feathers.
SECURITY GUARD	Meet me outside the Hot Chicken Shop in ten minutes. I'll show you where I last saw Merlin. *(Hangs up.)*
ASTRID	The Hot Chicken Shop! Aunty Rhoda vanished there!
NARRATOR	Astrid rides her Harley to the Shopping Centre carpark. Her number plate is EGGS-PERT. She sniffs around the back of the Hot Chicken Shop.
ASTRID	Bones in the rubbish. Clues to my ... ex relatives. *(Dog on leash drags Security Guard across stage and sniffs at Astrid who holds up her ID card.)*
SFX	*WOOF WOOF WOOF*
ASTRID	This is my ID. And here is a photo of Merlin. Have you seen this man laugh before?
SECURITY GUARD	That's Merlin all right. He was next to the perfume stand in the mall yesterday. Is that right Rufus?
SFX	*WOOF WOOF WOOF*
SECURITY GUARD	What sort of chook are you?
ASTRID	English Sussex. See, I'm white with a black collar.

SECURITY GUARD	*(Pulling at dog.)* My dog Rufus has a collar.
ASTRID	I'm glad about his collar. Ahhhhhh *(Guard Dog chases Astrid, who runs past stalls of perfume, and girl who squirts them.)*
PERFUME GIRL	'Remember', 'Stop' and 'Forget' are on special this week. Yesterday I squirted the aftershave called 'Forget!'
ASTRID	I can smell 'Remember' on my beak. Wonderful! It works.
NARRATOR	Astrid grabs a bottle of 'Stop' and squirts it at the dog who stops and sits.
ASTRID	*(Panting)* Sit.
PERFUME GIRL	Give me back my bottle of 'Stop'.
ASTRID	*(Giving back bottle.)* Thanks for the clue. Did you squirt 'Forget' yesterday when Merlin was around?
PERFUME GIRL	Yes. Until the guard complained. The rabbit in the magician's hat was coughing.
ASTRID	Flopsy? That rabbit is always complaining.
SECURITY GUARD	Merlin was here for two shows, so he was sprayed a lot with 'Forget'.
ASTRID	Maybe Merlin 'forgot' his sense of humour because of the spray?
SECURITY GUARD	Like a poison?
ASTRID	When I was in the lab, I was sprayed with something by mistake. That's why I can read things. And sometimes read clues to people's minds. Do you remember if Merlin laughed in the first part of the first show?

SECURITY GUARD	Yes, he did. But by the end he was grumpy. And so was that rabbit.
ASTRID	Perhaps Merlin forgets to find things funny when he's been sprayed. Perhaps that's how he lost his sense of humour.
SECURITY GUARD	How are you going to get it back?
ASTRID	Same way I stopped Rufus. An antidote. The opposite perfume.
NARRATOR	Astrid thanked the guard and left quickly. She could feel an 'egg' coming on. Eggs are her ideas. She's careful about where she leaves them. At home, she checks for messages. Chooks Anonymous is quiet.
FLOPSY	*(Swaggering on stage.)* I hear you've been running around like a headless chook.
ASTRID	*(To audience.)* For such a beautiful bunny, Flopsy can be SO thoughtless. A rabbit like her doesn't think. Her words hurt. I can see that picture in my mind. Headless chook. That picture worries me more than chicken recipes on the internet.
FLOPSY	Have you found Merlin's sense of humour? It's nearly time for the Magic Show. I can't remember what time we start.
ASTRID	Did you get squirted by 'Forget' perfume yesterday?
FLOPSY	Yes. But I can't remember days and times now.
ASTRID	*(To audience.)* That's a clue! Flopsy never did have a sense of humour, so she couldn't lose it. But maybe she 'forgot' other things. Maybe the perfume spray affects her in a different way?
FLOPSY	If you're not careful, Merlin will sell you at the bird auction. But I can't remember when that is.

ASTRID	Thanks. You always say such kind things.
MERLIN	*(Grumpily)* Hurry up. Time to go on stage.
ASTRID	*(Dialling)* Hello Perfume shop? Could I have a bottle of Remember delivered urgently? Yes. Credit card. *(Astrid sprays Merlin with 'Remember' and he starts to smile and joke.)*
NARRATOR	They do the card trick. Merlin gives Astrid the clues by the way he asks the question. Is it a red card? Means it is red. Do I have a red card? Means it's black. *(Astrid sprays Flopsy with 'Remember' perfume.)*
FLOPSY	I remember that the show starts at 3.
ASTRID	Merlin's show is already started and you're on NOW!
FLOPSY	*(Hurrying)* And the bird auction is Friday 13th.
CHICKS CHORUS	No thanks.
INSPECTOR CLUES	You should have asked for my help in solving the mystery. Remember is a French perfume.
ASTRID	It's an aftershave.
INSPECTOR CLUES	*(Shrugs)* Same thing.
CHICKS CHORUS	Congratulations. We heard you'd solved the mystery of Merlin's lost sense of humour.
ROOSTER	Should try farmyard perfumes like 'Grain' or 'Mush'. Joke!
NARRATOR	They're taking 'Stop' and 'Forget' perfumes off the market for more lab testing.
SFX	*RING RING RING*

ASTRID It's my agent.
 (Answers her mobile.)
 Hello Ben. Got another job for me?

BEN Carrot the Parrot has lost his voice.

ASTRID I'm not surprised.

Discussion Starters

- Prepare your director's advice for the cast: In this script, Astrid the Mind Reading Chook does have dialogue to speak and doesn't just mind read, so what must the actors and the director agree upon? How can a chook use a mobile phone? Can it peck or text?

- Writing dialogue for a character who is a chook and also mind reads is a challenge. There's a difference between writing 'thoughts' in a story and speaking dialogue on stage for a bird like Astrid. So the purposes of narrator and chorus are useful to link the action in a script. There needs to be action which could include chasing or dancing or singing. Otherwise the writer has to invite the audience to 'go along with the fiction' that Astrid can speak. As director, what will you suggest? What if the actors disagree?

- Satire is used in 'Sleuth Astrid: The Mind-Reading Chook' showing that fantasy still needs logic. The writer has to structure the story so that cast, motives and action sound credible within that story and the actions are possible on stage. The technique of satire is often to make suggestions on how attitudes might be changed or problems in a community solved, but presented with wit. It is laughing 'together' at our foibles, not laughing at each other. Savage satire aims to destroy the subject. Gentle satire aims to solve the problem together for audience and actors. Discuss satire and its use.

Activities

1. Write your own mystery script to perform by yourself or with co-writers. Mysteries depend upon:
    - Place (setting)
    - Person (characters or suspects)
    - Plot (what happens next?)
    - What's your mystery? E.g. something lost or thought to be lost?
    - How was the mystery committed? Clues?
    - When did it happen?
    - Where did it happen?
    - Find out the facts. Google or visit the place

- By telling, acting or reading, share your version of the story
- Motives: Why did the person do that? Why did the sleuths want to find out?
- Choose an unforgettable title
- Design your cover or program

2. Prepare some sound effects (SFX) for your production. This may include music or prerecorded audio. Sometimes you may wish to prerecord all the dialogue so that cast can concentrate on action, especially if you've only got a small group.

3. Write your own Sleuth Astrid book or script.
   Choose a title. Play around with ideas that could be clues to what the story is about.
   - SpellChook? (Plays on the idea of Spellcheck)
   - Sleuth Astrid and the Missing Word
   - Hi-Tech Speller
   - Spells, Speller and Sleuth Astrid
   - Or choose titles for each chapter or scene and then take the best one for the book title

   What goes wrong? What is the setting? TV game show? Emergency sign in a farmyard? Hospital? Supermarket? Spelling bee?

   How does Sleuth Astrid get involved? What is the mystery she has to solve? Plan a twist for the ending.

Sleuth Astrid: The Lost Voice of the Grand Final

A play about celebrations and the influence of sport

Script adapted from Hazel Edwards' eBook series, *Sleuth Astrid: The Lost Voice of the Grand Final*, illustrated by Jane Connory.

Cast

- Narrator – can have a giant 'prompt' book
- Astrid – a chook sleuth with a mobile under one wing, who pecks on latest device or microphone. Carries ID card
- Rooster – thinks he knows everything
- Footy player
- Agent Ben
- Carrot the Parrot
- Assistant Coach
- Hen Chorus
- Red Lips TV Assistant
- Speakeasy – the bartender and his guard dog
- Orange Lips Radio Assistant
- Beak the Bridegroom
- Bride

- Voice Coach
- Clara the Clairvoyant Chook
- Clues the French Chick
- The Runner (Optional voice over)
- Chorus
- Fans (any number)
- Optional non-speaking parts:
  - Footy player who hobbles
  - The Creepy Crawlies team
  - Feline team
  - Technical crew

Props

- ID tag for Astrid
- All Entry Pass
- SFX – Harley Davidson motorbike noises

Setting

- Farm yard
- Footy ground
- Speakeasy bar
- Studio

Sleuth Astrid: The Lost Voice of the Grand Final Script

NARRATOR	Grand Final is one of those special days. For months, footy fans look forward to the Grand Final, especially if their team is in the Finals.
SFX	*TEAM FOOTY SONG (Make up own.)*
FOOTY TEAMS	*(Speak together)* We're the footy teams. We wear our colours. We sing our team songs. We talk about our players' injuries.
HEN CHORUS	Will our best player be fit in time? *(Footy player hobbles across stage.)*
HEN CHORUS	Not looking good.
ROOSTER	I like the team with my Rooster colours.
NARRATOR	Rooster thinks he's boss of the yard. But the hens are the real players. They know all the farmyard gossip about who is doing what.
ASTRID	*(Shrugs and speaks to audience.)* As a hi-tech chook, I know stuff Rooster doesn't. I also work part-time as a sleuth.
ROOSTER	*(Strides across yard.)* Do you follow soccer?
ASTRID	*(Shakes head.)*
ROOSTER	Do you follow aussie rules?
ASTRID	*(Shakes head.)*
ROOSTER	Do you follow rugby?
ASTRID	*(Shakes head.)*
ROOSTER	Then why are you going to the Grand Final?

ASTRID	Working there. Here comes my Agent Ben.
AGENT BEN	Astrid, are you ok to work on Grand Final Day?
ASTRID	Does that mean I get in for free?
AGENT BEN	Only if you're wearing this special ID tag. *(Hands over ID tag and All Entry Pass.)*
ASTRID	Thanks. With this all entry pass I can get into any stand, even into the training area. This ID tag says 'Visitor: Special Security'. I'm on the job, but I'm not telling Rooster. The hens will tell him the gossip soon enough. He'd be green with envy and that won't match his club colours. *(Hen Chorus gossip as they leave stage. Rooster follows, eavesdropping.)*
AGENT BEN	Usual pay rate? Z-Tek games?
ASTRID	Thanks Ben. Bye. I love getting paid in hi-tech toys. I like being a hi-tech hen. I can peck very fast on my screen. Chickens are ordinary, but I'm special. Ever since that accident in the lab I've been able to read minds. I'm excellent at finding things but I choose my jobs. No more Hot Chicken Shop commercials. It's no mystery what happened to my Aunty Rhoda in there, she became a Special Sandwich with lettuce, mustard and pickles. And my uncle is now a duster at the Feather Bed Shop, so I won't act in bed shop commercials either.
SFX	*RING RING RING*
ASTRID	Hello, Astrid here. *(Pulls Z-com from under wing.)*
AGENT BEN	Astrid, it's Ben again. I've got another job for you. This is NOT a Chicken Shop acting job, okay?

ASTRID	Where is it?
AGENT BEN	The Sports Centre. Part of the Grand Final on Saturday.
ASTRID	Yes. Hens in the farmyard have been talking about it, so has Rooster.
AGENT BEN	The Coach has got Grand Final fever.
ASTRID	Old news! What's the job?
AGENT BEN	Something is lost again. You did such a good job last time finding Merlin the Magician's lost sense of humour.
ASTRID	*(Laughs)* Merlin needed his laugh back in time for his 3pm magic show at the shopping centre. He got it. I look for clues and I keep my eyes to the ground. Most people don't notice a chook who's just pecking around.
AGENT BEN	You found the laugh.
ASTRID	Who's the client this time?
AGENT BEN	It's Carrot the Parrot himself. He's lost his voice.
ASTRID	That's no mystery, he probably wore it out.
CHORUS	*(Speaks to audience.)* Carrot is one of those parrots who is always talking. Parts of him are orange like a carrot, however he says he's exotic. No garden vegetable colours for him. We think he's just orange-carrot coloured. Very noticeable, especially when he yells at you.
AGENT BEN	The Birds team are in the finals and Carrot is the coach. He says they need him at the ground to tell them what to do.
CHORUS	How did Coach Carrot tell Ben if he lost his voice? Email?

ASTRID: I use Chook mail myself on my Z-com.

CHORUS: Do you watch TV Sports? Coach Carrot is always being interviewed on 'expert' panels. Carrot talks all the time about football, himself or at special events at which he is Master of Ceremonies.

AGENT BEN: Now he can't talk or tell players what to do, so he sent an urgent email.

ASTRID: When did he lose his voice?

AGENT BEN: Before he got up this morning.

ASTRID: Does he know where he lost it? Or why?

AGENT BEN: No. That's why you've got the job of finding it. The Voice of the Coach must be at the Grand Final.

ASTRID: What about my fee?

AGENT BEN: D'you want the usual?

ASTRID: Yes please. The latest versions of e-games like Leghorn, Eggs Galore or Find the Egg will be fine.

AGENT BEN: The voice must be found before Saturday's game. Also the Coach has an even more important speaking date the next day.

ASTRID: Sunday?

AGENT BEN: Yes. It's Bird of the Year Wedding.

ASTRID: Is Carrot getting married?

CHORUS: *(Muttering)* Who would marry Carrot?

AGENT BEN: Coach isn't keen on any of his footballers getting married on Grand Final weekend. The Bride wanted to marry at 2pm on the Saturday but the game was on the same day. Now the wedding will be on Sunday instead and Carrot is supposed to be the MC.

ASTRID	Who decided the wedding was on the Sunday?
AGENT BEN	The Coach.
ASTRID	Why do the wedding party do what the Coach says?
AGENT BEN	Because Beak The Bridegroom is also the captain of the football team. They need Beak for the Grand Final. He has to help his team to win or else …
ASTRID	Who do you barrack for? The Birds?
AGENT BEN	*(Laughs)* How did you guess? What are you doing?
ASTRID	*(Googling 'Voice,' 'Lost' and then 'Birds coach.' next, 'Voice coach.')* If I visit the football training ground, maybe this time Carrot will listen to me?
SFX	*HARLEY DAVIDSON MOTORBIKE NOISES*
ASTRID	Keeping my helmet on, just in case.
CHORUS	Last time a low flying bird dropped on Astrid's Z-com. Good luck or what? *(Footy teams doing training exercises. Fans wave streamers, balloons and posters with their favourite players.)*
FANS	*(Cheering)* BEAK!
ASTRID	Beak is very popular with the chicks.
CHORUS	Birds team is training so hard. This is just a practice and the fans still cheer.
ASSISTANT COACH	*(Yells)* Go back! Keep on your player. *(A runner goes onto the field with messages about tactics.)*
FANS	Photo please. Autograph my hand, Or my leg, Or my sleeve.

CARROT	*(Signals to the Assistant Coach who is too busy to notice. Carrot is cross and sends the runner on field a lot.)*
ASTRID	*(To audience)* How can I find out the facts from Carrot? Sign language? But he's not deaf, just voiceless. Carrot can hear people, they just can't hear him.
	(Puts Z-com screen under Carrot's beak.) Tap. I'll ask a question. You peck an answer.
	(Carrot is a bad speller. His 'score' becomes 'sore' and 'hamstring injury' becomes 'ham-bone.' Voice becomes 'vice.')
	(Carrot shakes his head.) I can mind read, but I get lost in Carrot's murky mind which is full of 'I' and has no room for anything else.
ASTRID	Open your beak. Let's look at your throat.
FANS	What are you looking for?
ASTRID	Not sure. D'you think you should go to the hospital Carrot? See the eye, nose and throat doctor?' *(Carrot shakes his head.)*
ASTRID	Carrot, where did you talk last? *(Carrot keys some places.)*
CHORUS	*(Reads them aloud.)* Sports Centre Talkback Radio TV Studio panel Speakeasy
ASTRID	I'll use my Z-com map to find the places. I'm going to solve the mystery of the lost voice. Lost property first.

SFX	*MOTORCYCLE NOISES*
FANS	The lost property office is at the sports centre. There are umbrellas, shoes and sports gear.
ASTRID	But no clues to a lost voice.
CHORUS	Let's read Carrot's list again ... Sports Centre Talkback Radio TV Studio panel Speakeasy
ASTRID	What is a speakeasy? A café? A bar? A fast food place? Judging by the name, you should be able to speak easily there. First, I'll check the henhouse. It's the gossip centre of the yard. The hens know everything.
HEN CHORUS	Cluck. Cluck Cluck.
ASTRID	Excuse me hens? Do you know a place called The Speakeasy?
HEN CHORUS	Yes, we decided not to go there for a hens' night out before the wedding. We don't drink homebrew. Cluck Cluck Cluck.
NARRATOR	The Speakeasy is one of those rough, farmyard places. According to the hens, the Rooster went there occasionally for a drink of grain-water homebrew. Hard drink was banned in the farmyard and speakeasy had its own homebrew and that attracted footballers and Rooster.
ASTRID	*(To audience.)* I have found Speakeasy on my Z-com. I'll eat at home first, eat before you drink is a sensible decision. Not that I was planning to drink homebrew at the Speakeasy anyway I am working.

I live in the bird yard. All kinds of birds rent a space, ducks, geese and even a swan who teaches ballet. I have my own loft where I keep my gear. There's a space for my bike and the sidecar.

While dinner cooks, I try Chooks Anonymous. You can leave a question, other people read it and they leave answers. I've keyed in, 'Lost voice belonging to Carrot the Parrot. Please contact Astrid the Mind-reading Chook'. I also typed in my link. I hope someone leaves me a clue before the Grand Final.

HENS CHORUS	Something's burning!
ASTRID	Dinner! Grainburgers with farm dressing and … burnt mush!
SFX	*RING RING RING*
SPEAKEASY BARTENDER	
	(Known as SPEAKEASY.)
	Are you the chook looking for the voice of the Coach?
ASTRID	I'm Astrid the part-time sleuth. My client has lost his voice. Have you heard that voice recently?
SPEAKEASY	Yes. Last night.
ASTRID	How do you know it belongs to Coach Carrot the Parrot?
SPEAKEASY	Because he was here, warning us not to serve his footballers.
ASTRID	Where?
SPEAKEASY	At The Speakeasy in the lane.
ASTRID	Which lane is that?
NARRATOR	Even a mind reader can't always get it right.

SPEAKEASY	The one on the side lane, behind Main Street. I'm leaving in half an hour. If you want to chat come over now, I'm the one with the guard dog.
ASTRID	*(Scans Carrot's face onto Z-com for easy ID.)* The Z-com clips on the handlebar. My number plate is EGGS-PERT.
SFX	*MOTORCYCLE NOISES*
CHORUS	*(Astrid wanders around looking for the Speakeasy sign.)* Hard to find the lane unless you knew it was there.
SFX	A CREAKY DOOR
ASTRID	Any lost voices around here? *(Silence)*
SPEAKEASY	This is The Speakeasy. I'm the Bartender. In the olden days, drinking was banned so people used to slip in here for a drink of homebrew. It was called farmyard rot-gut. It's easy to speak when you've had too many drinks.
ASTRID	Did Coach Carrot come in here yesterday? Is he likely to drink much? He's always telling his players to lead healthy lives.
SPEAKEASY	Hard to see anyone in the dark here.
ASTRID	*(Switches on head light.)* Your dog has a very big mouth. Can you stop him sniffing my tail feathers?
SPEAKEASY	*(Checks ID.)*
ASTRID	I won't check your dog's identity. The other side of the bar is close enough.
SPEAKEASY	So what sort of chook are you?
ASTRID	I'm an English Sussex. See, I'm white with a black collar.

ASTRID	*(Shows the scanned 'mug shot' of Carrot.)* Do you know this Parrot? He's the Coach of the Birds who are playing in the Grand Final but he's lost his voice.
SPEAKEASY	I know that beak. He was here yesterday afternoon, complaining.
ASTRID	Did Carrot lose his voice here?
SPEAKEASY	Well, he used his voice here. He told us not to serve any drinks to his footballers. The Birds players had to be fit to play in the Grand Final. Our place was banned.
ASTRID	What did he say exactly?
SPEAKEASY	*(Shrugs)* Help yourself to any sound you like. Web cam has security shots and recordings of all our visitors. Take a copy if you like.
ASTRID	Thanks. *(Scanning)* Carrot repeated himself a lot, it's given me an idea. Usually I can feel an idea egg coming on. Carrot's voice must be recorded in other places where he had worked before. Talk-back radio must have recordings too. Maybe I could join together his second-hand words and phrases? And use them until the Coach's voice has returned. After all, Carrot did tend to repeat himself.
CHORUS	Eggs-xactly!
NARRATOR	The TV studio has see-through walls and shiny, slippery red seats. Chooks prefer feather not leather for their backsides. They are more comfortable, and there's less chance of them falling off. Astrid waits in the glassy room with all the mirrors and pictures of famous TV faces. Were they real or air-

brushed? Often faces did not match the voices...it's the same with birds and beaks. A red ON AIR light blinks. So much red in this studio.

ASTRID
How well do you know Carrot?

RED LIPS TV ASSISTANT
Well enough. He's so untidy, I'm always having to send on autographed footballs, match fixtures or tickets that he's forgotten.

ASTRID
Do you remember if he spoke much during the TV interview?

RED LIPS TV ASSISTANT
(Nods)
He was on the panel at the beginning of the first show. Bit of a problem with the sound quality. Director hit the mute button with his backside. An accident.

ASTRID
(Aside to audience.) I'm beginning to think that TV studios are uncomfortable places for bottoms.

(Turns to face Red Lips TV Assistant.)
So Carrot was speaking at 12 o'clock? Was the show live-to-air or pre-recorded?

RED LIPS TV ASSISTANT
(Pauses) Well, the audience thinks it's live, but really we record the day before ... just in case ...

ASTRID
In case of what ...?

RED LIPS TV ASSISTANT
Bits need to be edited out.

ASTRID
You mean swearing?

RED LIPS TV ASSISTANT
(Nods) Or if the match has an unexpected result.

ASTRID	Thanks for your help. *(Checking Chooks Anonymous.)* Only one email about football tips for the Grand Final. Birds are favourites.
SFX	*TALKBACK RADIO*
ASTRID	Talkback radio next. Maybe I could get a recording of Carrot's voice from their files? By law they have to tape it, just in case any callers say anything rude. There's always a 30 second delay before it goes to air.
ORANGE LIPS RADIO ASSISTANT	Carrot had a voice coach, to improve his voice when he first started on radio.
ASTRID	Do you know the name of the voice coach?
ORANGE LIPS RADIO ASSISTANT	*(Shakes her head.)* But you can listen to the replay.
ASTRID	Thanks. I'll google 'voice coaches' first. Here's one.
SFX	*RING RING RING*
ASTRID	*(Best voice)* Hello. Can you have a coach for a coach? If the footy coach has lost his voice, do you offer help?
VOICE COACH	That's an unusual request.
ASTRID	Carrot the Parrot just wants to be able to yell again at the footballers.
VOICE COACH	Oh, my last parrot client wanted to sing opera.
ASTRID	Carrot is a football coach, not a singer.
VOICE COACH	Sorry, I don't think we can help Carrot. But maybe we can give you a free lesson?

ASTRID	Do you think I need it?
VOICE COACH	Mmmm.
ASTRID	Maybe I could act as Carrot the Parrot and be his Voice, even if I look nothing like him. I have Chooks Anonymous again. Nothing! Could I find a look alike? A speak-alike? Someone to act as Coach in his place or with his voice? Ben must have some Carrot look-alikes on his agency books. I call him.
SFX	*RING RING RING*
ASTRID	Ben, do you have anyone who could act as Carrot at the Grand Final? A look-alike? He doesn't have to say anything. All coaching will be prerecorded.
BEN	Yes, I do have one.
ASTRID	Who?
BEN	You.
ASTRID	Forget it. *(Hangs up.)*
SFX	*RING RING RING*
ASTRID	Good afternoon hens.
CLARA THE CLAIRVOYANT	Heard you found the voice of Carrot the Parrot, I knew you would.
ASTRID	Well I've found the Coach's voice, recorded in the TV studio and on Talkback radio. But unfortunately it's not working in his throat.
ROOSTER	So you're the hard-boiled detective?
ASTRID	He makes the same joke every time we meet. It isn't funny. I just wish my Z-com would ring so Rooster'd think I'm busy, but it doesn't.

CLUES THE FRENCH CHICK	*(Smiles)* If you can't fix something, change the way you look at the problem. Carrot was here and he told Rooster a practice wedding joke, so he still had it then. Would you like some help with this case?
ASTRID	*(Shakes beak.)* Not yet, thanks. Unless it's a French mystery, where you have to speak French, I think I'm better at the job.
CLUES	Some birds don't talk at all. Parrots can be trained to say 'hi' or bark like a dog.
NARRATOR	Others are multilingual in French, Spanish and Chinese; Some go for walks like a dog, with their owner holding the leash. Others can sing opera.
ASTRID	Great, but Carrot just wants to get one voice back. His own.
ROOSTER	*(Interrupts)* Did you hear the news?
NARRATOR	He means the football news.
CLARA	I know. The Creepy Crawlies made it to the Grand Final. The Birds were so glad that the Felines got knocked out in the semi-final. The Birds wanted to play footy, not get eaten.
NARRATOR	The ROAR of the crowd was recorded on the Big Screen as Carrot led them onto the field for their victory parade. Carrot's Voice boomed from the recycled TV program tape.
ASTRID	I'd edited all his other coaching hints, plus his TV commentary. He mimed as if he were speaking. Then, up on the big screen, the Creepy Crawlies ran out, in time to their team's song.

NARRATOR	Later that afternoon it was a draw! The all female Creepy Crawlies drew in the Grand Final. Coach was speechless. Especially when he discovered next day that the bride followed that team! There's a rematch next weekend, but Beak is on his honeymoon and can't play.
ASTRID	Hi Ben, I've found the voice of the Coach.
AGENT BEN	Where was it?
ASTRID	In one way, the Coach's voice wasn't lost.
AGENT BEN	What do you mean? Carrot couldn't even croak. Are you trying to tell me that he's learnt sign language?
ASTRID	Carrot the Parrot had always had used sign language with his players. Some signs were very clear and a few were a bit rude. My mind-reading skills have been no use for this job. I must pay credit to the Hens, especially the French chick Clues. They told me about ...
CHORUS	*(Shout together.)* The Runner!
ASTRID	During a match, the Coach gives instructions to the players, via his Runner. The Runner goes and tells the player what to do. The Runner is called the Coach's voice. And he's been around all the time. He never was lost. The Runner was at the Grand Final. He is the Coach's voice. Are you still there Ben? So, although the Coach had a sore throat and couldn't talk, he still had a voice in the Runner. Of course, Coach also uses sign language!
AGENT BEN	But what about the wedding? How can Carrot MC the wedding? He can't have a Runner there.

NARRATOR	Astrid didn't tell Agent Ben, exactly what the bride had said about Carrot not being able to talk at her wedding. That would have been rude. Beak and the bride made other arrangements.
ASTRID	Me! Well, I can read minds and I knew they were going to invite me to MC their wedding, so I offered. No charge. They said I had such a great voice, especially after lesson 101 from the Voice Coach online. That birdseed wedding cake was memorable. And so were the speeches, especially Beak's to his bride.
NARRATOR	And who do they get to captain the Birds in the re-match? Well, that's another story.

Discussion Starters

- Why is football so culturally important in Australia? Some people say that football is like religion. Do you agree?

- Do you support a football team? Which one? Is it possible to support two football teams at once? What is your earliest football memory?

- Have you ever played a football or sporting video game? Does it come close to the real thing?

- Do footballers, coaches and sports celebrities have a responsibility to behave well off the pitch? Why is this? Why are footballers paid so much money? Are they worth it?

Activities

1. Prepare, as a group, a new character dossier. Create your new sleuth character for your own story set around your place.
   Can be human, animal, insect, or bird.
   - Name …
   - Job …
   - Skills: Is good at …, Is not good at …
   - Lives …
   - Favourite object …
   - Wears …
   - Owns …

   Draw this character

1. Explore different media to share your story or share this play.
   - Audio with SFX (sound effects)
   - Magabook (halfway between magazine and book)
   - eBook
   - Comic graphic novel
   - Dance interpretation
   - Cartoon etc

Contacts and Further Information

There are several topics and issues covered in this resource. If you, a teaching colleague, a student or school family needs further support we suggest you contact:

Beyond Blue
www.beyondblue.org.au | 1300 22 4636

LifeLine
www.lifeline.org.au | 13 11 14

More about eating disorders:

Butterfly Foundation
www.butterfly.org.au | 1800 33 4673

Inside Out | Institute for Eating Disorders
www.insideoutinstitue.org.au

More about conservation:

Greenpeace
www.greenpeace.org.au

WWF: World Wildlife Fund
www.wwf.org.au

Friends of the Earth Australia
www.foe.org.au

More about haemophilia and health:

Haemophilia Foundation Australia
www.haemophilia.org.au

World Health Organization
www.who.int

More about grief and bereavement:

Australian Centre for Grief and Bereavement
www.grief.org.au

GriefLine
www.griefline.org.au

More about inclusion and diversity:

Inclusion Australia
www.inclusionaustralia.org.au

Diversity Council Australia
www.dca.org.au

www.ingramcontent.com/pod-product-compliance
Lightning Source LLC
Chambersburg PA
CBHW050248120526
44590CB00016B/2267